LOVE YOU, SWEETIE

LOVE YOU, SWEETIE

Extraordinary ordinary true stories of one woman's quest to love, be grateful, and stop complaining

Beth Lambdin

Published in the United States by Beth Lambdin.

Publisher's Note: This is a work of nonfiction. Some names have been abbreviated to an initial to protect privacy.

The following have appeared previously, in slightly different form, in the following publications: "The Bike Ride: Before and After September 11," from the 2002 anniversary edition of *Voice of the Hill;* "Turkey Days," in *Holidays, Season's Greetings from Sunny Florida!, A Space Coast Writers' Guild Anthology;* "My Florida: Home for Now," in *Florida, Stories About Living the Good Life in the Sunshine State*, an anthology published by *Anthology Alliance;* "My Mother's Ring," "Waiting for Irma," "This World Will Break Your Heart," "A Death in the Family," "Mom and the Waitress," "Three Bras and a Bottle of Bombshell," and "A Sunday Evening with Dad," at BethLambdin.com, *Writing the Extraordinary Ordinary.*

ISBN: 978-0-578-52141-1 (hardback)
ISBN: 978-1-7360748-0-0 (ebook)
Library of Congress Control Number: 2020901809

for

Aunt Celie
1943-2018

Contents

Notes to the Reader

Since 2000, I've kept a record of what I read. My entries are simple and include the title of the book, the author's name, the date I finished it, a letter grade reflecting how much I liked it, and F for fiction or NF for nonfiction. In a tally, my reading habits skew to nonfiction by a ratio of about 3:1.

If I were to tally my writing habits, they'd skew even more toward nonfiction.

This got me to wondering: Just what is it about nonfiction—personal essays and memoir specifically—that is so appealing? Why is nonfiction what I mostly read, mostly write? What does it give me? What does it give other readers?

I imagine the answers are as idiosyncratic as those other readers. We are, after all, unique; and yet the same, too. And *that* understanding is at the heart of why I write what I write—mostly personal essays, casual autobiographical sketches, and short memoirish pieces—allowing me to tell stories with specific, personal, and unique details. Those details are like fingerprints touching each of my experiences, but also can be viewed through a broader, more universal lens, resonating with a wider audience.

We each contain a multitude of stories, so you might wonder: Why do I write? And why do I put my personal life out there to public scrutiny? In other words, why am I doing what I am doing?

Let's start with the first question: Why do I write? First and foremost, I write to make sense of a life, personal and public, which can both confound and delight me. I've stumbled down a lot of bumpy roads, kicking up a lot of dust before settling on writing: the therapy road, the booze-besotted road, the workaholic road—always looking for an ephemeral "something" that I felt was missing. I believe I've found that "something" with writing. My writing is a vehicle for understanding and transformation, which allows ease of travel down the road, which may still be strewn with obstacles, but now those obstacles feel more like adventures to experience than burdens to endure: I am no longer choking on the dust I kick up (on most days). All the bumbling and stumbling around I've done over my lifetime has undoubtedly helped set me on this path. Writing provided me with all sorts of *aha* moments and simultaneously left me with some regret, embarrassment, and shame. But this is also happening: Through my writing (and aging, too), my perspective shifts and evolves along with my craft. I keep enlarging my lens and seeing my life, and also the world in general, with different eyes—and a more compassionate heart (on most days).

I also write to make sense of things: a national tragedy (see my first published essay, "The Bike Ride: Before and After September 11," from the 2002 anniversary edition of *Voice of the Hill*), a cousin's tragic early death (see "Marjorie"), my mother's decline into Alzheimer's disease (see "Washing Dishes" and "Mom and the Waitress"). Also, there's the story in which I tell myself I can't dance (see "Laundry"), and another story of a disturbing exchange with a stranger I can't shake (see "My Florida: Home for Now").

Writing about personal stuff gives me a stress-release valve. No matter the circumstances (and believe you me, I don't always behave well or with equanimity), even in the midst of a stressful situation—lying face down with my breasts dangling through holes in the lab table waiting for a needle to pierce my delicate skin; waiting for a delayed flight with no explanation about what is going on; or seeing a voicemail that probably means someone I love has died—simply knowing I will have the opportunity to write about my experience gives me a level of acceptance that previously eluded me. I always think to myself, somewhere in the back of my mind, during these ordinary, everyday life experiences: *This will make a good story*; or, *Wow! That was a great thing that person just said, and it bears repeating*; or, *That was weird or funny*; or, *Someone else will relate to this*. Writing affirms that I am not alone in the world or even in that most dangerous of places—my own mind.

I write as though I am from both Gloversville and Broadalbin, New York, and I am, sort of. My family lived between the two towns. We had a Gloversville address and went to church and shopped there, a bigger community than Broadalbin, but Broadalbin is where I went to school and where almost all of my friends lived. In a way, Broadalbin was the emotional center of my youth.

You will note that certain people run through my stories. On occasion, I have referred to him or her by just initials to respect privacy. My husband, Jim, is a central character and comfort, and he appears in more of these stories than anyone else. (Attention-shy, he would appreciate the irony inherent in that.) However, while Jim is the central human character, he is tied with our animal companions, our three cats, for notoriety (and comfort, too). My mother, both dead and while alive, also figures prominently, as does my father, or the "old guy," as he calls himself. Brothers Bill and Tom pop up, Bill more frequently than Tom, which is reflective of our real-life, out-of-the-book relationships. And then there is everything else: good friends, a casual acquaintance who offers a port in the storm, and total strangers who say something shocking (see "Reading Mary Oliver at 4:30 a.m." or "My Florida: Home for Now"). Finally, there is the endless bounty of nature—the Atlantic Ocean and its inhabitants, the flat-out-splendid Florida sky, the diverse Florida fauna and birds, and the foothills of the Adirondacks, especially spectacular in autumn.

As Nora Ephron said, "Everything is copy."

My stories do not always flow in chronological order, which was a deliberate decision, and most accurately reflects my writing process. I started some of these essays many years ago, while others are more recent. Many contain elements of the past as well as contemporary-life snippets and references. Memory is a fickle, fractured medium, at least for me. I aim for the essays to flow and be illuminated by their order, something akin to a thoughtfully curated show of paintings, where the exhibit gains even more power by the specific placement of the works next to each other.

This collection of stories contains common themes: love, loss, humor, issues of aging and health, animal joys and sorrows, rituals and rites, the power of books, politics, culture, nature, and love, again—always love—in its everchanging guises. While not always tidy, I aim for some connecting threads to run through this collection. Here's one example: As you read, you will see I am, indeed, a deeply flawed human being, *and* a human being who is often acutely aware of how and when I get it wrong. Like everyone, I am full of contradictions. I am a human being who wants to do better, who is deeply committed to spiritual evolution, and yet seemingly stuck in some negative traits (like complaining). Perhaps, ultimate salvation (if there is such a thing) lies in the hard-won place of being more present, more in the moment, more compassionate, and more forgiving of self and others: progress, not perfection.

Another thread seeks to identify how we are all more the same than different at our core, giving me hope (and maybe you, too) for our continued existence on this fragile yet resilient planet. This thread tugs at the notion that we can create outsides that better match our wiser, more tender insides.

Finally, there is a thread composed of those unique moments that were happy surprises I didn't even know had registered in my heart and mind until I sat down and started writing (see "Marjorie," "Mom and the Waitress," "This World Will Break Your Heart," and "Love You, Sweetie").

It seems I've offered at least partial answers to those questions I posed at the beginning: Why do I write? Why do we read what we do? Why should you hang out with this book? Maybe all those answers boil down to this, though: To forge stronger connections and relationships with self and others, and to put ourselves in the way of those totally unexpected moments of grace.

Connections. Relationships. Moments of grace that fall like a gentle rain washing everything shiny new again. May my stories—the stuff of ordinary life—resonate with you, and perhaps bring forth your own oh-so-human and heartfelt moments, strengthening the bonds between us.

Washing Dishes

Daylight is fading to dusk when I turn left into the driveway of my parents' house. As I glide down their driveway, I see my mother in the soft glow of the kitchen window. The window is over the kitchen sink and, although I can't see her hands, I know what she's doing. She's washing dishes.

She is an eighty-two-year-old woman and has washed a lot of dirty dishes over her lifetime. I perform a quick calculation and figure she has stood there, in that exact spot, with yellow rubber gloves snapped over her hands, and plunged into soapy dishwater at least 50,000 times over the forty-seven years that this kitchen has been the beating heart of her home. Bathed as she is in the fading light of the day, she could be performing a religious rite—and maybe she is. At the very least, it's a routine, and one I hope is a comfort to her now that Alzheimer's disease has ravaged much of her brain and made mince-meat of most of her routines. She can't do a lot of things these days, but damn, she can still wash dishes—so she does. And I bet, too, that the fragrant, warm, soapy dishwater feels good on her arthritic fingers.

I can't see her clothing, but I guess she is wearing an apron, one that either she or my father pulled out of the metal drawer in the bottom of the stove that always squeals when you pull it out—maybe her favorite apron, the one with a hem of purple lilacs. But since donning clothes, let alone tying a knot, is way beyond her capabilities now, it is likely my father helped her put it on and then smoothed it over her ample belly before looping a lopsided bow in the back.

This kitchen is familiar territory, important for Mom. My parents bought this house in 1960. It's a modest split-level with an eat-in kitchen and one small window over the sink, which looks out on the driveway. This driveway was originally gray gravel, little pellets that crunched under my boyfriend's car tires and made it impossible to slip in unheard and unnoticed past my curfew. Along with those late, wild nights as a teenager, gone too is that noisy gravel, replaced with a smooth, black asphalt that allows infrequent visitors like me to glide in almost silently.

If Mom looks up, she'll not only see the driveway but the front lawn, a broad, overgrown expanse dotted with markers of my childhood. In the past, she watched us play out there as we smacked a bat against a softball. Sturdy pines then and now tower over shorter trees. One of those pines, our first base, is a survivor of our thoughtless tugs as we stripped its limbs bare of needles in our mad dashes to safety. The crabapple tree, smack-dab in the middle of the yard in a straight line from the kitchen window, was second base. My mother always had a fondness for that tree, which my father planted specifically to remind her of the dogwoods she loved in her native Maryland. It's a resilient old codger that still bursts into vivid pink blossoms each spring, despite years of neglect. Third base was a pole-support cable on the edge of our property, which doesn't seem like the smartest choice, in retrospect. Only home base is missing, a particular patch of trampled grass with edges that grew straight up like my older brother, Bill's, crewcut.

I start to wave to my mother, a simple act I've done a thousand times. I wait for her to look up, to wave back, but she doesn't, and my hand falls to my side.

Coming home is tough. It evokes a lot of mixed feelings, and before I enter my parents' house, I pause for a few minutes on the flagstone walk to collect my skittering emotions. As I stand there, I notice the rhododendrons that line the walkway, which my mother so carefully tended for years and years, have now grown wild and tangled—just like I imagine the synapses in her brain have done. But, while they remain unpruned, the plants still thrive.

I wish I could say the same for my mother. It seems like mostly I tally what she no longer can do these days. Here's a partial list: She can no longer dress herself, tell the time, name the day, or the season, or how many kids she has. She can no longer play bridge or look up words in the dictionary that lies open on its stand in the dining room. She can no longer apply deodorant, tie her shoes, name the president (maybe a blessing?), drive, write a check, cook, or bake the pecan sticky buns she is known for throughout the county—nor can she any longer taste and enjoy food.

The rhododendrons' flowers are still beautiful, however, even in their wild, untended state. Maybe they are an invitation to see beyond all the losses and to instead focus on what is beautiful. Is there still beauty in my mother? Yes! And it's pretty easy to see. Through the window, I notice how her reddish-gold hair glints in the sun and how her skin looks so soft I want to reach out and stroke her cheek.

Gumption gathered, I go in to find Mom rinsing dishes. As I glance at the sink, my first thought: relief that they are plastic. Hooray! My mother has hit a crappy trifecta. Along with Alzheimer's disease, she has Charcot-Marie-Tooth disease, a genetic neurological disorder which, combined with arthritis, has devoured much of the muscle in her hands. Mom and ceramic do not go together.

But Mom and washing dishes do. Although these health challenges have dimmed her natural brightness, she still washes dishes (and sometimes even remembers to add the detergent). Why does this activity endure when so much else has fallen away? Is washing dishes a patterned response, an ingrained motor memory, like riding a bike? Or does this ordinary act persist for another reason? Does it comfort my mother?

I have to wonder if she inherited some "clean" gene directly from my Pennsylvania Dutch grandmother. But

I suspect the roots go back even farther, to earlier clean-freak ancestors in Germany and Holland. I bet you could eat off the floor in my ancestors' houses with no worry of illness or disease—if you felt so inclined. But sometimes, there is that skip in generations when it comes to genetic markers. While I have inherited my mother's myopia (nearsightedness), I haven't inherited her varicose veins. I also don't express much of a "clean" gene (in fact, just the opposite) and can only hope that the same holds true for any Alzheimer's markers.

In our family, Mom's always been the chief dishwasher, but I don't think she necessarily envisioned me, her only daughter, in that role. However, growing up, I was often by her side as the dish *dryer*, which I hated and saw as a colossal waste of time. Since she insisted my two brothers take their turns in the dish-drying rotation, I was on duty only every third night. That left time for more important things, like making mischief with my friends. Anything, anything at all, was preferable to spending time with my mother drying dishes. Although, for a few years in high school, I strategically used dishtime to my advantage. I learned it was better to "dish," that is, to confess my "sins," and especially my boyfriend, Vince's, "sins," before she heard about our latest transgressions from the local gossip at her Friday morning hair appointment.

Nonetheless, dish-drying time with my mother was fraught with tension. We wore ruffled aprons with floral prints, not jailbird black-and-white stripes, but we were prisoners nevertheless, clueless about how to bridge the gap between us. The apron strings were merely functional—any deeper ties long before severed—so I naively believed.

As a teen, I was absolute in my convictions. "When I have my own house to run, I'll stop this idiotic practice of drying dishes. For God's sake, it's so stupid!"

"Don't say God, Beth," my mother replied in an even tone.

"They'll dry on their own!" was all I could muster in response. And, they do. True, the glasses and silver (rarely used) sport water spots, but who cares? My grandmother (who also ironed sheets and underwear) probably rolls over in her grave as I say this. *Sorry, Grandma.*

The unusually heavy dish-washing/drying times were during holidays or other special occasions when my mother insisted on using her good china and silver and then refused to put any of it in the dishwasher. One Thanksgiving, rushing to dress for a date, I dropped the delicate, china gravy boat, and it shattered on the floor. My mother burst into tears as I stood there, feeling awful, wondering how I could ever put all the pieces back together again. I couldn't, of course, it was beyond repair.

While at first glance, you may think that my mother and I don't look much alike physically, we do share that severe myopia I mentioned earlier—an inability to "see" except for what is right in front of our faces. But with or without glasses, nearly everyone recognizes that I am, indeed, my mother's daughter: We share light eyes, fair hair, and many of the same gifts (extreme sensitivity), and many of the same demons (extreme sensitivity).

Now, my mother is just a year younger than her mother was when she died. With every passing year, she looks and moves more like my grandmother—only with that never-dyed, reddish-brown hair—instead of gray. They share broad hips and a soft belly, long, skinny, gnarled fingers on the end of reed-thin arms, and an unsteady gait on feet numbed by neuropathy. But there's one difference that shrieks out to me: My grandmother's mind was sharp as the proverbial tack until the day she died.

"She is one of our kids, isn't she?" I heard my mother ask my father during a previous visit. "You are my daughter, aren't you?" she asked me when I hugged her goodbye. "Yes, Momma, I am." Now that the doors have slammed shut in my mother's memory and I am on the outside, I regret all those missed chances to connect more deeply with her.

Is it too late? It might be. But maybe I just can't see what's been there all along, just beneath the surface in all that soapy dishwater. Maybe, if I squint hard enough, the foam will part and spell out some sappy soap-opera sentiment about true and enduring love.

Nah, I don't think so. But I am starting to understand that it never was about the words and that my mother and I have always been connected—superficially, at least, by those blessed apron strings—for better or worse. I wish I'd been struck smarter decades earlier and realized that all those times in the kitchen with my mother when she had the full range of all her faculties were the "better" ones. It just never entered into my teenage brain that, in a few decades, I would regret my self-centeredness.

Like a pigeon imprinted with a homing instinct, I return to my parents' house, again and again, searching for something—and on this trip, I finally find it. Alzheimer's disease, an unwelcome interloper, lurking in the house, messing with my mother's brain, did me a favor by stripping away the superficial parts of my relationship with my mother, the intellect and words and years of accumulated armor, freeing me to see beneath the surface to what is true and timeless: the love we share. Unlike apron strings, our heartstrings, although as tangled as her synapses, as unpruned as the rhododendrons, can never be cut. Heartstrings are not superficial.

I love my mother, and I tell her so.

On my next visit, when my car glides down the driveway, I'll look for my mother in the kitchen window. I hope she will be there. If she is, I'll join her in the kitchen, tie our apron strings with perky bows, pluck a clean dish towel out of the squeaky stove drawer, and take my place next to her at the kitchen sink. Then, my mother and I will do the dishes together one more time.

Shattered Glass

They say adolescents have impressionable minds. I've always wondered exactly who *they* are. But never mind, I had one—an impressionable mind, that is. An impressionable mind I bombarded with words from the pages I read by the faint glow of the greenish-yellow nightlight stuck in the wall socket of my pale pink bedroom wall after my mother ordered, "Lights out!"

I count my lucky stars I grew up in a house of readers. My mother mostly read magazines: *Good Housekeeping, Reader's Digest, McCall's, Time,* and *Newsweek,* and newspapers; the local ones, *The Leader-Herald* and *The Amsterdam Recorder,* as well as *The New York Times.* I leafed through the magazines, but it was my father's books I devoured: *Some Call It Sleep, From the Terrace, Couples, An Appointment in Samarra, The Seven Minutes, Butterfield 8, Herzog,* and *In Cold Blood: A True Account of a Multiple Murder and Its Consequences,* by Truman Capote. That last one was what critics would call a real game-changer.

That Capote.

He wrote the tragic, true story of the quadruple murder of the Clutter family in a spellbinding, novelistic style. It is a disturbing story of a fine, upstanding, Methodist family who had the terrible misfortune of colliding with a pair of ex-con drifters in the early morning hours of November 15, 1959, in Holcomb, Kansas.

Much of the subject matter in those books (especially the sex) was beyond my experience and, therefore, beyond my understanding. I was genuinely perplexed by sex in those days. I believed you could get pregnant by kissing. Imagine being that naive! Imagine how I felt after my first kiss at age thirteen during a game of "seven minutes in heaven!" It happened at an unchaperoned party in a rambling yellow house, where the girls threw one of their shoes into a big pile, and the boys pulled out a shoe from the heap at random. Then the boy, the shoe, and the owner of the shoe skulked off to a private corner.

I remember my shoe that night. It was no svelte glass slipper, but a sturdy tan-and-green number with black shoelaces. I recall that the tan part was corduroy. It was a comfortable, sensible, low-heeled shoe, which felt snug on my totally average, size seven-and-a-half foot.

That first kiss was from a cute guy, who, at seventeen, was too old for me. His name was Frank. It wasn't particularly heavenly (more peculiar than erotic), and I didn't care for his tongue wriggling around inside my mouth. I was perplexed by boys in general, and kissing specifically, and *especially* the sex I read about in my father's books—still a couple of years away from any direct experience.

But that murder in Kansas stamped an indelible impression on my young psyche. Murder in Kansas I got.

The Clutters were an ordinary, God-fearing family: parents, Herbert and Bonnie; two adult daughters, Eveanna and Beverly, no longer living at home; and two teenagers who still were—son Kenyon and daughter Nancy. It was Nancy's murder that haunted my dreams.

After reading *In Cold Blood*, I begged my father to replace the glass window by our front door as it would be so easy to smash, effortlessly allowing bad men to clomp up our stairs in heavy work boots, snatch my brothers and me from our warm beds, and do unspeakable things to us. My father laughed at my fears and did nothing.

I grew older as all kids do, except for Peter Pan in J. M. Barrie's world, and no longer had to hide the fact that I was staying up late, past my mother-mandated bedtime to read adult books. I grew up, unlike Peter Pan or Nancy Clutter or her brother, and I grew to like kissing and sex. And, on one occasion, I stayed up all night reading a book in one sitting. The book was Thomas Harris's *The Silence of the Lambs*, an excellent example of that rare occurrence when a movie adaptation does the book proud—thanks to three performances for the ages: Jodie Foster as Clarice Starling, a student at the FBI Academy with a troubled past; Anthony Hopkins as Dr. Hannibal Lecter, a brilliant psychiatrist with a taste for human flesh; and Ted Levine as Buffalo Bill, a serial killer with a fondness for female skin. Talk about indelible impressions.

As I've grown even older (if not downright old), I have never been accosted, despite my youthful fears. None of the houses I've lived in has ever been broken into. However, mischief-makers did break into my fire-engine-red Honda CRX one night while parked out in front of our house on busy 11th Street in the Southeast Quadrant of Washington, D.C.

In the morning, while retrieving the newspaper from our postage-stamp of a front yard, I noticed my car door was slightly ajar. On further inspection, I discovered my CDs had been rifled through and strewn across the front seat. But, after a careful inventory, I realized none had been taken. I guess he/she/they were not big Mary Chapin Carpenter, David Bowie, or Paul Simon fans. But, really, how can anyone not like Paul Simon's "Diamonds on the Soles of Her Shoes?" Come on! I felt more insulted than violated by this snubbing of my musical tastes.

Except for that one minor violation, there has been no demonstrable, clear evidence that I am in danger in the wee hours. Still, that early conditioning is powerful, and I never fully relax, keeping one ear cocked on high alert, especially while the rest of the household slumbers, Catsby-cat, and Jim snoring away. This hypervigilance has become a habit, and I suspect I've altered my brain chemistry over the years, making deep sleep elusive. When I finally close the book I'm reading, click the lamp off, futz with the pillows and covers, right before drifting into a fitful sleep, for just a minute or two, I listen for the sound of glass shattering in the still of the night.

Turkey Days

Half a mile down the road from where I grew up in rural Gloversville, New York, there once was a restaurant that had a turkey farm on its property. The coops behind the restaurant were filled with plump, White Holland turkeys, noted for their white plumage in days of yore. But these restaurant owners raised and slaughtered them exclusively for their tasty meat. This meat was especially savored on the grandest turkey day of all, Thanksgiving. For six consecutive years in the seventies, I served the hungry customers who packed the restaurant on Thanksgiving. Though the turkey farm and the restaurant would eventually close, the connections forged there would outlive the bulldozer and endure to this day.

A Brief History

Our family moved to Gloversville late in 1959, when I was five years old, in the midst of what would turn out to be a typical, bitterly cold winter. The skies hung low with metallic gray clouds waiting to dump snow, which, subsequently, froze hard enough to support our kid bodies as we crunched across it to wait for the school bus at the side of the road. We left behind a compact, "starter" home on Brook Road, in a suburb of Baltimore, teeming with other young parents and baby boomer kids who furiously pumped the pedals of their red-and-white bikes and trikes as they careened down the sidewalks.

My parents loaded up their offspring, a boy and a girl (me!), and our mongrel dog, all black except for round, brown eyebrows, with the singularly uninspired name, "Blackie," to pursue a better job for my father. A physicist by education and an engineer by training, my father, had grabbed an opportunity to broaden his responsibilities. The financial incentive, which doubled his current salary, sealed the deal, and off we went.

Like our new house (that now would be marketed as "mid-century modern," but then was a plain old split-level), the restaurant with the turkeys had a Gloversville address, but a Broadalbin phone number, which was just four digits. Ours was easy enough to remember, 5242, but not as easy as theirs, 4321. Although I rarely called the restaurant before I worked there, I was fascinated by its countdown symmetry, which I noticed on various printed advertisements as I grew up.

However, those simple four-digit codes assigned to our locale were limiting and meant that we could essentially only call within Broadalbin's population of about 2,500 without paying an extra fee. According to an out-of-date phone book, we did have access to several other tiny communities, like Day and West Center, Osborn

Bridge, and Parkville, but that wasn't much of a benefit since they rested as ghost hamlets at the bottom of the Sacandaga Reservoir. The reservoir was created by flooding the valley back in 1930 in an effort to control the pesky Hudson and Sacandaga Rivers, which would sometimes jump their banks to inundate those villages. Flooding the valley, however, displaced and destroyed those long-standing communities and carried unintended consequences, including irritating my mother decades hence by offering only a minimal telephone-call zone without incurring a charge.

The restaurant was formally named The White Holland House, after those White Holland turkeys, but we always called it "The Turkey Farm." The restaurant sat at the corner of Routes 29 and 29A. Our house, up the road and on the left on the way to Gloversville, sat squarely on 29A—which no one ever called 29A. Instead, it was simply Turkey Farm Road.

Walt and Arlene Coons owned and ran The Turkey Farm. They married the day before the Japanese bombed Pearl Harbor in December of 1941, and the couple opened the restaurant in 1948, with six tables for customers. One of their twin daughters, Judith, said her parents specialized in "everything turkey." Boy, did they! The restaurant served all turkey all the time: the traditional turkey dinner, of course, and entrées like turkey chow mein, turkey croquettes, turkey salad, and turkey à la king.

A Favorite Place

We were regular patrons—my parents for Friday night dinner after my mother's bridge group, and our whole family for lunch after church on Sundays.

Shortly after we moved to New York, my parents shopped around for a church home. They joined a Presbyterian Church because they felt an affinity with the young, progressive minister, Reverend Reed. Unfortunately, he died of a heart attack a few years later. While the minister who replaced Reverend Reed was more than adequate, he never inspired my parents in the same way, and it was easy for my father to fall away. While my mother hung in there devotedly for more than fifty years, my father's attendance became more erratic. He would come and go, returning at one point to add his lovely tenor to the choir (which was always in need of more men), but leaving again to stay home to listen to Reverend Charles Barker and his broadcast from Alice Tully Hall in New York City's Lincoln Center on Sunday mornings. Barker was a minister of Religious Science, founded by Ernest Holmes, whose spiritual, philosophical, and metaphysical beliefs aligned more with my father's than those held by the Presbyterians.

But even when Dad wasn't attending the service, he'd drive us the 5.1 miles to church, drop us off, and then return about an hour later to pick us up. We'd swing by the corner store at West Fulton and Main to pick up *The New York Times*, always held in reserve for us, and then head off to The Turkey Farm. After glasses of golden Sauterne for my parents, root beer for my brother, Bill, and a Shirley Temple for me (with two maraschino cherries that I always gave to my father), we chowed down on a repast of all things turkey: chow mein for my father, croquettes for my mother, a turkey dinner with trimmings for my brother, and a turkey sandwich on white bread with lettuce, tomato, and mayo for me. Then, once Dad paid the bill—always leaving a generous tip and plucking a toothpick from the shot glass by the cash register—we wandered out back to visit the turkeys, a flurry of squawking, strutting white plumage. The mere sight of the birds filled me with delight, and I shrieked those ear-piercing squeals unique to little girls. I never once gave a thought to the turkeys' reality; that their days were numbered, and I had just consumed (and enjoyed) one of their relatives.

In 1961, our family grew by one when my parents added a baby boy, Tommy. The restaurant grew too, in much greater numbers and over several more years, eventually seating about three hundred customers. A cozy lounge served golfers from the course across the road, and a large dining hall attracted a particularly robust August crowd headed to the thoroughbred racetrack in nearby Saratoga Springs.

An Extension of Home and a Community

We Lambdins were loyal customers over the next decade. In some ways, The Turkey Farm was an extension of home. It was close by, and we knew the Coonses well. Walt and Arlene built our house after bulldozing away thick tangles of woods to erect a trio of similar split-levels, and my parents initially rented it from them—with an option to buy, which they did after six months for $19,000.

After all those years of patronage, we also knew the older, stable waitress staff, as well as the young people who worked there after school, during the summers, and on Thanksgiving Day. So, it was a natural place for me to seek employment. I started there when I was sixteen, first as a bus girl, and then as a waitress when I turned eighteen and could legally serve liquor in New York. I was diligent and motivated, always looking for things to do when business was slow. I wiped down table legs, filled salt and pepper shakers and ketchup bottles, and put away clean dishes still warm from the drying racks.

I liked the people I worked with, the "oldsters" and the younger contingent, like me. We were a mix of veteran employees and temporary help. Perhaps there were tensions between the groups, between us kids going back to high school or off to college in a couple of months and the regulars who did this for their living, but I didn't feel much of that. Though there was a waitress who remarked on more than one occasion that my mother was naive, in a tone that implied Mother was like some hot-house orchid from an earlier era, and it did not feel like a compliment.

Perhaps, being a middle kid sandwiched in between two brothers (Bill three years older, Tom seven years younger) helped me develop the skills to get along with everyone. That may have helped explain why, senior year in high school (when I longed to be voted "best dressed"), I was instead voted "best all around." I was disappointed. Was I really that superficial back then? At any rate, I've since learned that demonstrating a strong work ethic and making an effort to get along with everyone tends to garner respect. I worked late at The Turkey Farm, I came in at the last minute if someone was sick, and I rarely complained about anything. Toss all those traits in a blender, hit mix, and out comes a fairly likable human being—or at least one not too objectionable.

The veterans, the "career" waitresses—Marge, Ernestine, Helen, Sylvia, and Ermenia—were older women, with hair dyed dark red or brown to cover gray, and bodies still trim from the physically demanding work, except for Ermenia, who was short, chubby, and never hurried. Siggy, the bartender, had a hitch in his step like Walter Brennan. The cooks, white dish towels slung over their shoulders to mop up sweat, barked, "Yer order's up," as they turned back to stir deep pots of steaming turkey soup and yank trays of yeasty rolls and roasted turkeys out of the industrial-sized ovens.

There was an easy camaraderie among my contemporaries, high school and college chums waiting on tables and washing dishes. The bus and waitstaff were always female, and the dishwashers always male and darling, despite sporting dorky hairnets. The dessert girl, my classmate Valerie, had lustrous jet-black hair and built-up muscles from scooping ice cream. She sliced generous triangles of tall, quivering, lemon chiffon pie with a graham cracker crust (always threatening to topple over), and squirted peaks of whipped cream atop strawberry shortcakes in clear-glass dessert bowls. The desserts made you want to shout, "*Voilà!*" when she set them on your tray, looking almost too good to eat. Years later, at the Corcoran Gallery of Art in Washington D.C., gazing at Wayne Thiebaud's paintings of pies, I flashed back to Valerie serving up those gorgeous confectionary masterpieces.

In 1972, at age eighteen and a college student, I was promoted to waitress. Hooray! That provided the opportunity to earn even more money for college expenses (and clothes) than I made as a bus girl clearing and cleaning tables. It also meant continuing to work on Thanksgivings, just like I did in high school, but now on holiday breaks from college in Maryland.

Thanksgiving was obviously a big deal at the restaurant, the finale for the season, and the place was always packed—reservations a must. On Thanksgiving, only turkey dinners were served, always family style, always as much as you wanted. But it wasn't a gluttonous gorgefest. There certainly was plenty of food served, all the usual stuff: plump turkey legs, mounds of dark meat piled next to white meat, gravy steaming in white porcelain boats, stuffing, mashed potatoes, green beans and mushrooms, carrots and peas, rolls and sweet buns, and those gorgeous house-made desserts. But, generally, one refill was all that was requested.

Friday Thanksgivings

For six years, my family stopped celebrating Thanksgiving on Thanksgiving Day to accommodate my work schedule at The Turkey Farm, shifting our own turkey day to Friday. Sometimes my mother invited her unmarried bridge partner, Grace, and at times she asked my bachelor Uncle Tom, who taught religion at Harvard, to join us for the holiday. Uncle Tom would ride the bus over from Cambridge. However, he refused to stay on until the closest station in Amsterdam, which was more convenient for pickup by my father. Instead, he chose to get off in Schenectady, which always irked my mother—along with his cigarette smoking—which stunk up the house, the stench lingering long after he'd gone home.

On those Fridays following the fourth Thursdays in November, I'd whip up a batch of daiquiris in the blender, heavy-handed with the rum, and we'd eat the delicious food my mother made for us. "Excellent meal, Betty," my father would say, his praise genuine. We'd finish with pumpkin or apple pie and crème de menthe glinting green in delicate crystal as laughter rang out around the dining room table. Even my naturally serious mother would tell an amusing anecdote or two, her speech slightly slurred as she felt the effects of the liqueur.

Eventually, the meal would come to a natural conclusion, and we'd heave ourselves up from the table. The menfolk would waddle to the living room to plop into cushy chairs and watch football (their combination of obliviousness and entitlement irking me more and more with each passing year), while my mother and I (and Grace, if present) would clear the table and take our customary places by the kitchen sink to clean up. My mother washed, and I dried, stacking the clean dishes on the kitchen table. Then, right before we untied our damp aprons and slung them over the back of the kitchen chairs to dry, we'd put the good dishes back into the china cupboard and slip the silver back into their velvet sleeves until the next day-after-Thanksgiving Thanksgiving.

Illusions Shattered—Plan B

I was not so consciously grateful on those Thanksgivings back in The Turkey Farm days. Perhaps that goes with youth—with not yet suffering the inevitable losses of aging. But I do know I was grateful for the job. And I think the bosses appreciated my dedication, although their emotional states were often opaque. The running of the restaurant was first and foremost a business, however, and one summer, they didn't hire me back when business was slow, which surprised me. In retrospect, it makes perfect sense. Of course, they would give preference to the veteran staff, who counted on the jobs for their livelihood. But I was shaken when my summer plans went awry. Still, the season was short, and I needed to make money for college expenses. I quickly formulated a Plan B.

So, at the start of the summer of 1973, I applied for a job at the local mill in Broadalbin, on the edge of the fetid Kennyetto Creek (which has since been cleaned up) with my best friend, Holly. But since Holly didn't meet the factory's weight requirement of 120 pounds, I went on my own. I joined the regular employees, punching the clock at 7 a.m. to start a soul-sucking day of refinishing furniture for college dorm rooms. I sweated my butt off in a non-air-conditioned hellhole, tipping large chests of drawers on their sides to slap on stains—which couldn't have been healthy to breathe in for eight hours a day with our non-masked noses—but that's what we did. Back at college, I would never look at a chest of drawers in the same way again.

On the mandatory breaks, the men walked like zombies over to the men's room and the women to the women's room to sit on wooden benches adjacent to the smelly toilets. They would eat snacks or lunch and smoke cigarettes. I sat in silence, not having a clue as to what to say. The regimentation of the day, the punching of a time clock, the required breaks, made me feel like I was stuck in a straitjacket, and I tamped down any natural exuberance that threatened to bust out. The easy camaraderie and bantering I had engaged in at The Turkey Farm did not translate to the mill. Maybe that was due to the incessant racket in the place, which made conversation nearly impossible. Or maybe there was a chasm I simply did not know how to cross. No one was unpleasant or overtly hostile, but our exchanges rarely extended beyond superficial pleasantries. Maybe the others knew I was a short-timer and not worth any personal investment.

My body ached constantly. But I quickly toughened up (and lost weight). I'd come home, eat dinner, and as the light drained from the sky in the early evening, I'd fall into a dreamless slumber, while outside my window, whippoorwills sang and bats swooped, snapping up mosquitoes.

I didn't realize it then, but looking back, I see that those men and women I spent my days with had gained my enduring respect. They worked hard, physically demanding jobs, which aged their bodies, making them stooped and twisted, and prematurely etching their faces with deep grooves that I imagine Dorothea Lange would have loved to photograph. Today, I better appreciate the toil of factory and millworkers, partly thanks to the evocative work of poet Philip Levine in his collection *What Work Is*, as well as the experience I gained from that challenging summer job of long ago. I was too self-referential to see much value then. Still, I do know that their silent stoicism and limited employment opportunities were powerful incentives to stay in college. "Education is power," played in my head on an endless loop.

The Turkey Farm and the mill were alike in some ways. They both buzzed with activity, and there was always something to do. But my schedule at the mill, and especially the 7 a.m. start, was a brutal grind. My eyes stung and were shot through with streaks of blood that summer. I looked hungover. I wasn't. I was too exhausted to go out at night and drink; even falling into bed early, I never felt adequately rested. By contrast, at the restaurant, the workday never started before 10:30 a.m. for lunch duty, and even later, when I was scheduled for dinner. More sleep put a spring in my step.

So, when business picked up at The Turkey Farm, and I was hired back, it was like the door on my jail cell swung open. I traded in stiff denim jeans, stained T-shirts, and steel-toed work boots for a white uniform my mother somehow always got the gravy stains out of, and white, thick-soled nurse's shoes—without an iota of regret.

But I also experienced a subtle, new wariness about The Turkey Farm. A certain naiveté had vanished. I felt betrayed they hadn't hired me back immediately that summer. Wasn't I part of the family? I learned then that business needs trump relationships.

A little less a child, a little more a grown-up, still, I was grateful to be back at The Turkey Farm that Thanksgiving. It mattered to me that my customers were happy. I liked anticipating their desires. I liked feeding people, and I liked getting paid for doing it.

Although the whole area was economically depressed in 1973, lousy tips were unusual on Thanksgiving. My customers tended to be quite jolly, even before downing cocktails on the holiday. They tipped generously, and I took great delight in stuffing my tips deep into my uniform pockets, savoring the final tally for later. At home, my mother would click down the recliner's ottoman to set her purple-streaked, varicose-veined legs and feet on the floor, lean in, and watch me count my loot. It was always a good haul on Thanksgiving—and it was a satisfying way to spend the holiday.

Cycles Repeat—Until They Don't

Then, after that turkey-eating-extravaganza Thursday, The Turkey Farm shuttered its doors and windows.

The owners drove south to Florida to relax, play golf, and escape the chill of a harsh winter until the spring when the cycle began again—which repeated for many years until Walt and Arlene retired and their daughters took over the business. Over time, though, the restaurant's popularity faded, and The White Holland House closed for good in 2009, the building razed a few years later—and The Turkey Farm faded into history.

But Turkey Farm connections endured. For a time, before Arlene died in 2009, she and my mother shared a room at the local nursing home. Both had dementia, both had not a clue as to who we were, but those two old ladies got along just fine with each other. I like to think of them sharing meals, maybe even chowing down on turkey.

And at a high school reunion, held on a chilly, rainy night in 2013 for the classes of 1972, 1973, and 1974, Kevin, the master of ceremonies, an affable guy I'd played drums with in band, asked all present who had ever worked at The Turkey Farm to gather together for a picture. Just a little over forty years later, the decades dropped away as nearly a dozen of us jostled for position, squished together, and slung our arms around each other. Then, someone, maybe it was Valerie, yelled out, "Say *turkey!*" as we smiled for the camera.

The Reunion

The reunion invitation hits my email inbox in early March. I hear the *ping* a room away. I open it, read it, and immediately RSVP *Yes,* without hesitation—a bold, decisive move. But as spring turns to summer and summer bleeds into fall, I start to doubt my decision. My surge of initial excitement morphs into, *What the hell was I thinking?* I have my own mixed experiences with prior reunions, so I ask friends and even casual acquaintances, "Have you ever had a good time at a high school reunion?" Rarely do they say an enthusiastic, "Yes!"

I am suffused with doubt, a quality I know well. Regularly, doubt leaks into my overly active mind and unsettles seemingly settled decisions. It's a sly adversary, doubt is. I can count on its corrosive nature like I can count on fall not really taking hold until after Halloween here in Cocoa Beach, Florida, a mere spit of land off the coast of Central Florida. My hopes rise on the occasional September morn when the temperature *almost* drops into the sixties, and the humidity *almost* releases its suffocating embrace for a few hours. Unfortunately, much like that cute guy in high school who flashed a brilliant smile my way, early fall flirts here are just a tease.

Still, despite doubt, something pulls me to attend this reunion. I've recently watched Michael Apted's *56 Up*, the next installment in his *7 Up* series, and perhaps that's influencing me. In the film, the now middle-aged men and women he's followed since they were seven-year-old kids are now the happiest they've ever been, more settled and more comfortable with themselves and others. Is that true about me? Is that true about my classmates, born smack-dab in the middle of the boomer years? My curiosity is piqued.

But more than curiosity drives me. Loss tugs, too, making me want to gather with old acquaintances. While I have experienced the inevitable losses that go with reaching a certain age, there have also been losses that don't follow any kind of natural order and have been particularly jarring and upsetting. Two ex-boyfriends have died: my first love, Vince, from a heart ailment, and another, Mark, who took his own life. And a classmate's niece, the principal at Sandy Hook Elementary School in Newtown, Connecticut, was murdered at the end of 2012. These untimely deaths rock any sweet notion that we are ever guaranteed anything—like a long life.

On the day Mark died, before I heard of his death, I threw up—a seemingly random bout of nausea that made no sense until I got word from a classmate several days later that he'd taken his own life. My reaction makes me wonder if Mark and I weren't still connected on some out-of-sight level, despite decades of separation. Might I still have other invisible yet powerful connections with my classmates, forged in those formative years growing up in upstate New York?

If I do go, this reunion will be the third I've attended since graduating in 1972. What I remember about 1972 is that we chose Jimi Hendrix's "Purple Haze" as our prom theme, convinced we were cool, hip, and unique. How many senior classes throughout the country thought the same thing? On the one hand, we were treated like adults. The voting age had just dipped to eighteen for the first time, and Richard Nixon won the presidency in a landslide. The legal drinking age was also eighteen, which was mostly irrelevant to me and my ilk. We'd been drinking in the local bars for a couple of years, with no one ever checking an ID. But, like Patti Smith chronicles in her book about her youth with Robert Mapplethorpe, we were also "just kids." Back then, I was consumed with myself, my friends, and sexy, dark-haired Vince.

Vince was a relentless, persistent seducer, and I succumbed to his considerable charms. He was also a lousy, unfaithful boyfriend. While my body thrilled to his touch, the rest of me was making plans to leave him and throw off the shackles of small-town life, which I did when I left for college eight hours away.

Ten years passed, and by the summer of 1982, when my tenth reunion rolled around, I lived in a tony suburb of D.C., in a not-so-tony house full of booze and music. On Thursday nights, I'd start the weekend early and pull the cork with a satisfying *pop* from the wine bottle, cigarette hanging from my lips. I'd turn on the stereo and blast U2's "I Still Haven't Found What I'm Looking For" before ending the night curled up on the couch with a cat watching *Hill Street Blues* on the television. My dentist, noticing the erosion of my front teeth, asked, "Are you sucking on lemons?"

That first reunion was held at one of the ubiquitous restaurant-bars ringing the Sacandaga Reservoir and is mostly a drunken blur. I imagine there was raucous laughter. I imagine I had a good time until the hangover hit the next morning.

Twenty years passed before I attended another high school reunion. It was 2002, and I lived eleven blocks from the U.S. Capitol and was adjusting to post-9/11 D.C. and the increased security: barricades, metal detectors, and bomb-sniffing dogs intended to keep us safe. Rather than comfort, I felt an omnipresent dread. When an ex-Army sergeant and his young protégé went on a killing spree from their blue Caprice and left ten dead throughout the Metro D.C. area, a friend asked, "What's left? Locusts?"

In an effort to recapture my youthful blondeness for the reunion, I highlighted my hair with subtle shades of yellow. I wore fitted black pants with a touch of spandex, a stretchy black turtleneck, and a hand-knitted (not by me) blue cardigan with pockets trimmed in black.

By then, I had forsaken the booze, not necessarily a good thing at a reunion. I ate mediocre food, drank tonic and lime, and strained to hear my classmates' stories over too-loud music. I tried to connect with one of my high school buddies, to reminiscence about drunken debacles, snowmobile crashes, and one weird afternoon when she and I divided our friends into groups of virgins and non-virgins. But, as the beer flowed and the volume of the music amped up, I felt increasingly alienated and decided to leave. At the exit, a classmate stopped me and said, "Bring your hubby the next time." I told her I would, while seriously doubting there would be a next time.

After eleven years, the reunion invitation *pings* in my email inbox. I am once again living in a small town, this time by the sea. There is still global unrest. There is still unrest here in the U.S., and Broadalbin, once the center of my universe, is now but a speck.

But that speck, like some freakishly strong magnet, pulls me home. On a Saturday night, with a misty rain fogging the windows, I tug a fitted, gray-knit dress over my head and snap the wide, black belt around my waist. I debate whether to string gray pearls around my neck or to loop a scarf to keep my neck warm. Since I can't make a simple decision, I wear both. I pull on a long, black cardigan to chase away the evening's chill and slip on my now-dead mother's wedding ring for luck. I do bring along the hubby, Jim, who buys a new pair of khakis for the occasion but ends up pairing his comfy, faded work jeans with an old cashmere pullover. He squeezes his wide, flat, size-twelve feet into tasseled loafers.

On the way to the reunion, expanded beyond my year to include the three classes that followed, I worry the slick, wet roads will be hazardous for the drinkers in the group. Then we are there, and Jim opens the door to the country club. Loud music smacks us in the face as we walk in. I swallow an impulse to turn and run as I am mobbed by classmates daring me to remember them. My saliva dries up, and I signal my husband for a tonic and lime.

Ten of us showed up that night from the class of 1972. We circle one big, round table, with my husband squished in between me and Joey, an affable guy who tells funny stories I suspect are embellished for effect. Would I really not remember him being dangled out the window by his feet before our seventh-grade history class?

Most of us had been together since kindergarten and still live within an hour of the school. Most have children, and many have grandchildren. I feel the familiar tug of the outlier (not a local, no kids), but instead of dwelling on how different I am from them, I focus on what we have in common—and our shared history. I settle into a comfort that has previously eluded me.

Before dinner, clanking a spoon to a glass to quiet the crowd, the master of ceremonies reads the names of the dead for each class. Some of us gasp, but many of us are silent as the toll rises. We totaled sixty-seven in 1972; now, we are fifty-seven.

In many ways, this reunion is just like the others: The food is mediocre, the music too loud for talking, the conversations often superficial. I listen to stories I don't remember. I yell myself hoarse to be heard and strain to hear. I hope my murmurs of assent and head nods are appropriate.

But this reunion is also different from the earlier two. This gathering is not lost in an alcoholic haze. It is not lost (at least, not as much) in a preoccupation with myself. This reunion is less about me, my solitary concerns, my idiosyncratic likes and dislikes, and more about the collective us, the reunited us, the more-comfortable-in-our-own-skins us, just like Apted's 56-uppers. And I realize that this *us* has a responsibility: not only to show up and swap funny stories, but also to honor our classmates who have died and to talk about the impact they had and continue to have on us, to celebrate their lives, and to celebrate the privilege that we, the living, have by growing older.

After four hours, as the alcohol flows and the reunion kicks into party mode, I am ready to leave. I hug my classmates goodbye. Then, as Jim and I step out into the damp night holding hands, I realize I haven't said goodbye to Mark, a cute guy I dated during a summer home from college. In the parking lot, I debate whether to go back. I almost talk myself out of it, but I don't. I turn around, walk through the door, and spot Mark near the bar holding a beer. I hug him. I have every reason to expect he has many years ahead of him, and I'll see him again at the next reunion.

But you just never know.

Marjorie

May 5, 1989, it rained hard, really hard. You may wonder how I remember what the weather was, all these years later. There are some people, like actress Marilu Henner, who can remember minute details of every day—yes, *every* day. She and about a dozen other people in the United States have a special ability called HSAM, or Highly Superior Autobiographical Memory. I am not one of those people.

I remember that day because tragedy struck.

It didn't just rain on May 5, though; it rained each of the four days before. Rain fell in great, gray dousing sheets of wet, and the wind barreled through my umbrella and blew it inside out as I scurried down the sidewalk. The rain fell relentlessly, a driving, soaking rain that left coffee-brown stains on my feet from the shoes that all that wetness ruined. I attempted to dry them out, but they were never the same; the ends curling up like the Wicked Witch of the West's. At work, we joked that maybe we ought to start building an ark.

The rain raised the local rivers, the Potomac in D.C., and the Patapsco and Gunpowder in Baltimore. The rain roused normally placid creeks out of their beds. Flash flood warnings beeped across my TV screen Sunday evening during *60 Minutes* on May 5. A promo for *News at 11* showed a dramatic rescue: Some lucky hiker dangled from a helicopter cable after being plucked from rocks that had become isolated islands amidst the raging waters of a rain-swollen river.

I felt uneasy seeing these images on the screen that night but had no inkling my cousin Marjorie would be a story in the news the next day.

On Monday, May 6, my phone rang at work, and as soon as I heard my father's voice, I knew something was wrong. He said, "I'm afraid I have some bad news. Your cousin Marjorie has been in an accident, and she's missing."

"Missing," I repeated dumbly. "What do you mean, missing?"

He told me Marj had gone out riding horses with friends the day before during a break in the rain. He said they followed a path along the Gunpowder River and decided to cross where they believed it was safe. Marj volunteered to attempt the crossing first, but about halfway across the river, her horse lost its footing and threw her into the water. Her friends told her father, who told my father, who told me that she caught and clung to her horse's tail for a few moments. But the horse didn't like her hanging on its tail and kicked her. She lost her grip, and the rushing waters carried her away. One of her friends dived in to save her. He had her in his grip for a second, but the force of the water was so strong it snapped the bones in his arm, and she slipped out of his grasp. He staggered back to the riverbank, where friends pulled him to safety. The horse clambered up the riverbank to safety, too. But the churning waters carried Marj away, while her friends and fiancé watched helplessly from the shore.

Such bad news is hard to process. In a daze, I hung up the phone and walked next door to my boss's office and told him what happened. He probably murmured comforting words, but all I remember is, "Go home."

I did, and once home, I turned on the TV just in time to catch the 5 p.m. news on Channel 2 in Baltimore. The reporter said, "The body of thirty-five-year-old Marjorie Lambdin was just recovered from the Gunpowder River. Ms. Lambdin drowned yesterday after ..." As I watched the screen, the rescue team pulled the zipper up to the top of a black body bag that held Marjorie.

I considered that so many conditions had to converge at just that moment in a really lousy way to take my young cousin's life. In the space of just a few minutes on a Sunday afternoon, my aunt and uncle lost their only child. Two ex-husbands, a fiancé, numerous professional colleagues, countless friends and extended family, two cats, two dogs, including her beloved white German Shepherd, Lenox, and her horse, of course—the horse that she'd rescued from being destroyed when it could no longer make money for its owners as a racehorse—all lost the present and future pleasure of Marj's company.

In the immediate aftermath, I wanted to blame Marj for drowning when I learned she did not know how to swim. I thought, *How stupid!* But everyone told me it wouldn't have mattered, given the ferocity of the raging waters. I wanted to blame the horse, too. It was the horse's fault, wasn't it? If it hadn't kicked her, she wouldn't have lost her grip, and if she hadn't lost her grip … and so on and so on. But it wasn't the horse's fault, of course. It was no one's fault. It was just a stupid accident. But it was easier to blame someone and be royally pissed than to drop into the deep, deep sorrow that yawned like a bottomless abyss.

I had just assumed Marj would be around forever. She'd always been hovering in the background like a guardian angel. She was a year ahead of me at the small women's college we both attended in Maryland, and she welcomed me as a nervous freshman. It was Marj who helped me get my first job out of college at a real estate company where she worked. It was Marj who helped me get another job when I left graduate school in Art History and was flailing around, searching for a "real" career. She convinced the director of personnel to hire me as a temp, which set off a trajectory of related personnel jobs for the next two decades. For a while, we both had offices on the same top floor of a former stable at Chestnut Lodge, a psychiatric hospital in Rockville, Maryland.

At the Lodge, Marj was a thin, svelte adult, with light-brown hair, frosted with blonde streaks, and gray-green eyes, having long ago left behind any tendency towards chubbiness. She had the kind of trim figure that wore clothes well, and she always looked smart, put together. She had impeccable eating habits. At lunchtime, I'd traipse down the hall with my bag lunch, pull out a shiny, red apple, and take big, noisy bites from it, while Marj pulled out a juicy, ripe peach from her bag and ate it with neat, efficient bites, never dropping a single, solitary droplet of juice on her starched white blouse. I marveled at her daintiness. Just how the hell did she manage to eat a ripe peach without dripping juice? I'd make a mess of it even standing over the kitchen sink wearing a bib. She had a talent, for sure.

But mostly, what we did together in her office at lunchtime was laugh—big laughs that rang merrily down the hall and forced me on more than one occasion to run to the bathroom so I didn't pee on myself. We laughed easily together; it didn't take much to set us off. I would bend forward from the waist, laughing, while Marj would bend in the opposite direction, throwing her head back and exposing her silver fillings.

At one of our infrequent family reunions, I caught Marj's eye, and we exchanged amused looks. We looked at each other, arched an eyebrow, and stifled chuckles when our fathers showed up nattily attired in their Bermuda shorts, dark socks, and sneakers, decades before that look would be hip in Brooklyn.

Lambdins like to laugh. My paternal grandmother was under five feet tall but had a big, booming laugh and a gift for merriment that she passed on to her four sons. Our fathers still get a huge kick out of the slapstick masters Laurel and Hardy. While Marj and I never really found them hilarious, we did love listening to our fathers fill the house with their riotous laughter when they watched the old black-and-white Laurel and Hardy flicks down in the basement.

We just kind of got each other—and since her passing, I've learned that those relationships are rare and something to cherish. I wish I had appreciated her more when she was here. I miss her and feel her absence profoundly.

After she died, there were two funerals for Marj, one in her hometown of Muncy, Pennsylvania, and one in Baltimore, for her colleagues and friends. I attended the one in Baltimore with an old boyfriend, Gray, who immediately, without missing a beat or taking a breath, said, "Of course I'll go with you," when I told him Marj had died.

Gray came to the house to pick me up before the funeral, and when I opened the front door, he stood there looking all handsome in khakis and a sports jacket, holding a plant bursting with green. A year later, on the anniversary of her death, I planted a rosebush for Marj, but it soon died. However, the plant Gray brought me on that sorrowful day not only thrived but survived much neglect and a move to Florida two decades later. It is the Arnold Schwarzenegger/Terminator of plants—seemingly indestructible. Or maybe it's blessed with some magical Marjorie dust.

At the church, my aunt and uncle stood in the vestibule, greeting mourners. My uncle, a Lutheran minister, seemed to be tending to us, the mourners, and I wondered if it shouldn't be the other way around. But there is no "right" way to be when you've just lost your only child. I hugged my aunt, and my legs started to shake uncontrollably. I was embarrassed, and the more I tried to stop it, the more I shook. It was one of the few times I've had absolutely no control over my body, and I clung to her and shook for what seemed like forever.

At the funeral, Marj's fiancé said to me, "She always felt all-powerful up on her horse." His comment made me wonder about just what an accident is, so I looked it up later. Webster's Dictionary defines it thusly: *An event occurring by chance or from unknown causes.* I asked myself: Was this accident simply the consequence of one moment of supremely lousy judgment? Was it simply an accident? Or was there some kind of invisible cosmic grand plan and her time was just up?

It sucked not having an answer to those questions. But, even if I had an answer, I was still stuck with the aftermath—the after-Marj. We all were. My father said, "All that potential lost. So sad."

The immediate aftermath was relatively easy. Friends said, "Stick to your routines." I did—I went to work. I fed my cats. I cleaned the cat boxes. I shopped for groceries. I (occasionally) cleaned the house. I did all those routine things, and yet I felt stuck in some kind of altered state. On the outside, I looked and acted normal. But inside, I had this gaping hole in the center of my heart. Friends asked, "How are you doing?" and I said, "Fine, okay, not too bad." No one mentioned my holey heart, and neither did I.

I learned to live with my Marjorie regrets. I regretted I had cancelled what would have been our last dinner together. I was slightly miffed about something Marj had said or done. I can't even remember the details, but I decided, rather than showing up and saying something and clearing the air and acting like an adult, to avoid the issue and nurse my resentment like a petulant child. I regretted that I said *no* to so many invitations she extended to me over the years. I regretted those missing hours of simply being in her company.

I wanted to make meaning of Marj's tragic end, and for months following her death, life was different. I was different. It was as visceral a feeling as the towel rubbing my skin after a shower. Many of life's petty annoyances—bloviating politicians, long waits in doctors' offices, droning noise, rude drivers—all that stuff felt unimportant, and I shed it easily, like raindrops sliding off a slick surface. I welcomed this new level of calm and serenity and vulnerability and hoped it would last.

And it did. And it didn't. Over time, I reverted to some of my old peevish behaviors, but Marj's death also jump-started an unstoppable mid-life awakening. I started to imagine a different life for myself, one where I didn't work fifty-hour weeks in a corporate environment that increasingly brought little satisfaction. I started to imagine work where I felt like I was making a meaningful contribution to the world. I started to imagine a life where I stopped coping with stress by drinking too much.

A year and five days after Marj died, I quit drinking. Two years after Marj died, I quit my well-paying corporate job and went back to school to study two years of pre-med science and math with the hope of becoming a psychiatrist. Three years after Marj died, I started dating Jim. Four years after Marj died, I failed to gain admittance to medical school on my first try. For a variety of reasons, including planning a future with Jim, which made a potential out-of-state move to go to med school less attractive (assuming I'd be successful on a second attempt to get in, a *big* assumption), I formulated a Plan B. I shifted to education, training to become a special education teacher, or what my future mother-in-law called my "downward mobility." But I was excited about working with kids, even if it meant a significant pay cut and being a newbie again in my forties.

My world kept growing larger—with new friends and stimulating work and a profound appreciation for the day-to-day wonders that are eternal, if we are lucky. I assume these are eternal: the beauty of a full moon stained orange hanging over the ocean's horizon, the ponderous progress of a giant sea turtle emerging from the sea to lay eggs, the way the light makes the bottom of a leaf shimmer with gold.

I miss Marj. I sometimes wonder what our relationship would be like if she were alive. She once told me she was really good at work but lousy at love. I wonder if her third marriage would have been a charm. I wonder what menagerie of animals she would be shepherding now. I wonder what great and small things she would be doing in her life.

Sometimes I have imaginary conversations with Marj. In them, I tell her our fathers are old men now and doing okay and that our mothers have died. I tell her that her mother is buried next to Marj's own grave in Mount Olivet Cemetery in Frederick, Maryland, and that her father frequently drives a few hours from his home in central Pennsylvania to visit them both. I tell her that while she may be gone, she is far from forgotten, and that my niece, Mary Marjorie, named for her, is an adult now and part of her legacy.

Sometimes I think I see her. My images of her are suspended in time, so she never ages. I recently saw a stranger on the street who looked so much like her that the sighting set my heart a-pounding, and I pivoted to do a double take before I saw that, no, it wasn't Marj.

I carried a heavy burden of grief, guilt, and regrets that weighed me down with sorrow and a deep, inconsolable melancholy at my core that kept a veil pulled over my eyes. But it must have just been one of those old-timey, little wispy half-veils, because one day it was gone. I don't know when it lifted, but it did, and I am grateful. I feared that the hole in my heart would never mend, but it has. Her death taught me I could survive, and even thrive, after losses that crater my heart so deep and wide, it's nearly impossible to think I could ever crawl up and out. Isn't the heart something?

I now live in a climate where it rains a lot. Sometimes, during the long, hot, endless Florida summer, it rains every day.

Like today. Great, gray sheets of rain fall from the heavens and fill the swales, the gullies beside our house dug for just that purpose—to catch the rain. I stop what I am doing and check to see if the cats, lounging out on the porch, are okay. I open the door. Two dart in, while one remains crouched under the table, using it as an umbrella, and I pause just to listen to the rain beat down, watch it streak the windows, and gush out of the gutters.

This rain evokes memories of Marj in gossamer snapshots. They are delicate, diaphanous things like the wings of butterflies. Best just to notice and let them flutter on by.

The Bike Ride:
Before and After
September 11

My morning bike ride is what's changed most since 9/11. But still, I ride. It's a habit I acquired after marrying Jim and moving from College Park, Maryland to D.C., and wanting to get to know the city more intimately (as well as getting some exercise).

It starts the same. I bike down East Capitol Street in the bike lane heading straight for the Capitol, choking on Metro bus fumes as the buses bully their way back into the flow of traffic. But when I reach the Capitol, the similarities between pre-9/11 and post-9/11 rides end.

Before 9/11, the Capitol Grounds welcomed me as an oasis of openness, beauty, and inspiration. I breezed through the entrance, waving to the lone guard in the guardhouse. The concourse was filled with scores of tourists and school children lined up for tours. I flew down the hill at twenty-five mph—the best part of the ride. I continued crunching down the gravel lining the

National Mall, passing the Smithsonian museums and the monuments with their ever-present tourists. The route was so familiar I failed to notice much about it, my senses dulled by routine.

Nearly a year later, the Capitol is a fortress of fences, barricades, and bunkers. It figuratively screams, *Keep out!* It's a challenge to find an open entrance to the grounds. Gun-toting guards and bomb-sniffing dogs are my morning greeters. I no longer have to swerve around tourists, suddenly stepping into my path, oblivious to me on my bike. The dominant human presence is the police; it's easy to maneuver around them, except on those days when they stop me. "The concourse is closed, lady. You'll have to leave." These words stoke the anxiety in my gut that has never fully subsided since 9/11 and make me wonder if another terrorist attack is imminent.

Don't it always seem to go that you don't know what you've got 'til it's gone? That line from Joni Mitchell's song "Big Yellow Taxi" runs through my mind. I've taken so many little things for granted: friendly waves from the Capitol police, trash cans in subway stations, concerts on the Capitol steps on balmy summer nights, celebrations on the Fourth of July free of metal detectors and frisks by armed guards, and museum entrances without signs that say, *Bag Searches Here.*

Pre-9/11 memories are fading fast, like old, poorly kept photographs. Flying down the hill is no longer possible. Now, it's a choppy affair. I get off and back on the bike. Then a few yards later, I get off and back on the bike again, and then again—mounting and dismounting, moving from sidewalk to road, road to sidewalk, negotiating the Jersey barriers, metal bollards, and construction equipment that block the hill.

Before I leave the Capitol Grounds, I glance up at the Statue of Freedom. She is nearly twenty feet tall, this classical figure wearing a crested helmet, resting one hand on a sword, and holding symbols of victory and the United States in the other hand, perched far atop the Capitol dome. Before 9/11, I rarely noticed her. Now, it's like I can't avert my eyes when I am near her; she compels me to look at her. For several months following the 9/11 attacks, she was encased in scaffolding. Coincidental timing, I'm sure, but the irony is not lost on me. Although her cage is gone, I imagine her weeping for all our lost freedoms. I wonder if these disturbing images will fade over time and if I will ever again feel free on the Capitol Grounds.

But 9/11 has also given me a gift, an enhanced acuity that I treasure. I no longer bike in a semi-comatose state. Now I look—really look—not just at the Statue of Freedom, but at all the monuments I pass on my daily ride: the Washington Monument, the Lincoln Memorial, the Vietnam Veterans Memorial, and the Jefferson Memorial, before making my regular stop in East Potomac Park to commune with George Mason.

Cast in bronze, George sits on a bench near the base of the 14th Street Bridge, deep in contemplation, taking a break from reading the volume of Cicero lying on his lap. His index finger holds the place where he paused in his reading. There are words inscribed on the stone wall behind George; they are his own. I take comfort in these elegant words that tell us that we are all born equally free and independent and have certain inherent natural rights, such as the enjoyment of liberty and the attainment of happiness and safety. These ideals, written in 1776, speak to the better part of me, to the better part of the collective us. I hope that we will find a way, post-9/11, to live up to them and that another lone biker will be inspired by them two centuries from now.

My Florida:
Home for Now

"**S**o, what brought *you* to Florida?" I sometimes get asked, since moving here from Washington, D.C. When I say, "My husband's job," instantly, I feel myself tumbling back into the sixties, my blunt bob morphing into a Laura Petrie flip, and my shorts and T-shirt into a plaid shirtwaist. That answer makes me sound like I orbit around my husband Jim (and maybe I do, to some extent), but I want to defend myself. Although, I don't really have to explain that I am no man's kept woman—in fact, Jim and I married in our forties, and I supported myself just fine until then, thank you very much.

But it *was* Jim's acceptance of a job at the Kennedy Space Center that precipitated our move—although there were likely several factors that made that new job offer particularly attractive. We had grown weary of city life after nearly thirty years, the noise and the traffic (always rated as among the worst in the country), and the extra level of effort it takes to live day-to-day in a major city bustling with tourists. Robust crowds dominate D.C., a good thing, overall, but still one yearns for just one spring when you can stroll around the tidal basin when the cherry trees snow pink blossoms in a brisk wind and not have to keep veering off the path to accommodate the distracted crowds. Hardly the stuff of "real" problems, yet day-after-day jockeying for space can wear you out.

And 9/11 changed D.C. for us. After the smoke cleared from the Pentagon, which we watched burn from our front stoop in our Capitol Hill neighborhood, Jim did his best to soothe my fears with statistics about how minuscule the likelihood of catastrophic disaster really was, how the numbers were with us and supported our continued existence. But the physical changes that went up in the neighborhood—the metal bollards in front of the Capitol, the closed streets, the re-routed traffic, bag checks in the National Mall museums, the increased police presence, the bomb-sniffing dogs, the warnings in the subway—none of them allayed my fears. And although over time the fear grew less acute, less sharp, it was still always there, a dull ache in the pit of my stomach.

Fear motivates—and narrows—the world to stark choices: fight, flight, freeze. We fled for Florida a few years later. Or did we? Maybe, just maybe, it was simply time to embark on a new adventure after three decades in familiar territory. Who in their right mind isn't seduced by beaches and palm trees?

Anticipation

While preparing to move to Florida, amidst the excitement that goes with embarking on anything new, three fears troubled my sleep, waking me with a jolt—always around 3 a.m. They were #1: storms; #2: bugs; and last but definitely not least, #3: the scorching heat. These were, of course, in addition to my general fear of the unknown, a big bag of slime that oozed anxiety about: leaving communities cultivated and tended for nearly thirty years, leaving family and aging parents, and entering a much more conservative area, where I knew not one single, solitary soul. Massaging my sore jaw after another night of clenching my teeth, I wondered: *How will we ever build a solid foundation on shifting sand and porous limestone?*

Despite the fears, we did it—we moved. On July 15, 2005, at a little after 6 a.m., on a D.C. morning already hot enough to prick sweat in our armpits, with our precious cargo, our geriatric cat, Hawthorne, meowing in a carrier that took up most of the folded-down storage space in the back of my fire-engine-red VW Beetle, we hit the highway, heading south.

Just Another Day in Paradise

The first year is like a vacation that doesn't end—all lush, fecund Florida vegetation, skittering lizards, nesting sea turtles, exotic birds, rocket launches, and nearly everything (doctor, baker, grocery stores, drugstores, art museums) within a thirty-minute drive. Traffic tie-ups, a ubiquitous feature of metropolitan D.C., are a rare occurrence on the Space Coast of Central Florida. But so is walking, except on the beach. "The sidewalks are coming! The sidewalks are coming!" I heard. I didn't know then that they wouldn't be laid for another decade. Until then, coherent, physical connectors in the neighborhood would either not exist or be pitiful, short stretches of concrete that ended abruptly in tangles of overgrown weeds and trash tossed from passing cars.

While Montana may be big sky country, Florida skies are no slouch. Here in Florida, the peach pinks and bruised lavenders, slate grays, and robin-egg blues are not just colors that pop on paintings by Stettheimer or Hassam or Hopper hanging on the walls of the National Gallery in D.C. Here in Florida, they hang overhead for daily delight. Nature is so generous to Florida.

Of course, D.C. has beauty too, spacious expanses of green along the Potomac and Anacostia Rivers, and iconic memorials and monuments that remind me of our best, aspirational selves. But D.C.'s lifeblood pumps on power and influence and work. Once upon a time, young and ambitious, I slipped into an obsessional work persona easily, perhaps too easily, donning navy and gray power suits and actual bow ties (for a blessedly short interval) while striving for some ephemeral *something* that would bring me ultimate satisfaction.

Florida, in contrast, nudges me to shift into a lower gear against a vibrant background of natural beauty.

Well, Maybe Not *Paradise*

Still, nowhere is perfect. While Florida has many Edenic characteristics, it falls short of Paradise. The salt air corrodes our car tires and windshield wipers and the convertible top of my Mazda Miata, leaving it dull and mottled. To wash windows is futility—the salt spray smears them in hours.

And, to state the obvious, it is hot in Central Florida (see anticipatory fear #3), a hellish state you can't fully comprehend until you actually experience it. Organic deodorant proves useless in this beating-down-relentless sun, and I don't even have to raise my arms to smell my stinky pits. Neighbors pull me into the shade and say, "Walk before the sun rises or after it sets."

Also, as I'd feared during those sleepless nights in D.C., the bugs (see anticipatory fear #2) are things of nightmares. Hawthorne dies, and we adopt a series of shorthaired cats, whose very life purpose appears to be wrapped up in hunting insects. For hours at a time, they crouch by a crack under the door to the garage, waiting for a bug to dart into their territory. Occasionally, one slips by them, somehow, and when I arise in the morning, there it is, a big, old roach, lying on its back, flailing its six legs in the air. "Ew," I mutter as I scramble in my comfy, old nightshirt, which is soft as a cotton ball and thin as a tissue, to find a broom and dustpan to sweep it up and toss it out the front door before it figures out how to turn over and scuttle away.

Then there are the termites. They swarm in the spring, which I didn't know until last year, when they displaced us for four nights, with our three cats, while the house was tented during fumigation. Four guys in long-sleeved shirts, khaki cargo pants, and steel-toed work boots clomped around on the roof and unfurled massive gray tarps (breaking enough tiles to catalyze a reiterative nine-month cycle of leaks and black mold that soured me on the Florida experience).

We moved here the year after hurricanes Charley, Frances, Ivan, and Jeanne wreaked havoc in the area (see anticipatory fear #1), and over the subsequent years, were lulled into complacency that, somehow, we were immune from hurricanes—until we weren't. Then Hurricane Matthew barreled through Florida, and we found we had underestimated just what it's like to live in a hotel room for several days and nights with three terrified cats and not know if we will have a home standing and habitable when we return. We huddled in the common area of the Homewood Suites in inland Maitland, north of Orlando, with others displaced from their homes, my phone lighting up with texts from concerned family members and friends as the storm bore down on Cape Canaveral. But a last-minute wobble spared us, and all we had to do was go to the local Dollar Store to buy a broom and dustpan to sweep up the mess the cats made with the litter before we checked out and returned to our still-standing, flood-free home.

Wherever You Go, There You Are

Coming face-to-face with my anticipated fears during the first year in this brave new world called Florida somehow made me more vulnerable and open. I wore my heart over my heart, sporting a favorite pink T-shirt with an appliquéd heart dead in the center—which I mended again and again as it grew increasingly holey—like some mad, obsessional tailor, refusing to give up on it and throw it away.

People are chattier in Florida. Is that a Southern thing? Regardless, over time, a new graciousness crept into my personal exchanges, and I factored in "chat" time at appointments. "Tell me what's going on with you," I say to my dental hygienist and settle in to listen as she punctuates the vivid descriptions of her twins' latest antics with merry laughs. And I stuck my toe in uncharted waters—here a writing group, there a new church, here a yoga class—looking for like-minded, like-spirited comrades in this grand adventure.

But a lot of those new experiences haven't stuck, for one reason or another. In the writing group, a guy detested pieces composed in the first person, and I, a personal essayist, felt his disdain when we read my drafts, and so I eventually left the group. The church's leadership cycled through a series of temporary ministers, and since I'd just gone through that in D.C., I didn't want to do it again here.

Perhaps most distressing of all is the resurgence of one of my worst character flaws—my habit of complaining. To my dismay, I discover that Jon Kabat-Zinn is right: *Wherever you go, there you are.* I am still me. In D.C., I complained about traffic and noise—all whirring helicopters overhead and screaming sirens on emergency vehicles careening down the street, and inconsiderate dog owners. In Florida, I complain about noise, just different noise—leaf blowers and lawn mowers, and weed whackers and buzz saws that lop off palm fronds and set my teeth on edge, and, still, inconsiderate dog owners.

Instead of the barking D.C. dogs jolting me awake in the early a.m. hours on the row-house porch next to our bedroom window, or trampling our newly planted pansies in the tree box out front, here in our new neighborhood, dogs bark at *all* hours. I slam the doors, clamp on headphones, and crank up a bamboo water fountain to shut out their infernal racket. Dogs roam off-leash on the beach, snuffling turtle nests and chasing shorebirds, pooping and peeing where I walk in my bare feet. Then there are the dogs that run up to me—sometimes playfully, sometimes not—which scares the bejesus out of me. Their owners invariably act oblivious that someone might find their dog's out-of-control behavior alarming and call out, "Oh, (Fifi or Fido or Bruiser) is friendly, don't worry." Grrr!

A wise woman once said to me, when I complained to her about people smoking in the bathroom at work, "There are naughty people everywhere." Indeed. Unfortunately, it is taking me much longer than I thought humanly possible to stop complaining, resisting, and wasting energy on things that are totally out of my control—and matter not one whit in the whole scheme of things. I am ashamed of my smallness, my pettiness. All I have to do is watch the news for five minutes to regain my perspective. I refuse to give in to my boorishness, however, and try to do my part to alleviate suffering in the world. And yet, my character flaws persist. A move to Florida can only do so much. *Wherever I go, there I am.*

March for Our Lives

Which brings us to the March for Our Lives—and guns, always a fraught topic eliciting strong emotions. On the morning of March 24, 2018, I laced up a pair of sneakers I rarely wear. I chose them for the additional support I hope they will provide for the approximately two miles that Jim and I will walk over the Eau Gallie Causeway, which spans the Indian River Lagoon and is about ten miles south of home. After speakers fire up the crowd, we join a couple of thousand others to raise our voices (and signs) for sensible gun safety measures. Shortly into the march over the narrow walkway, where we can barely fit walking side by side, my feet start to hurt—really hurt—so much so that it becomes hard to focus on anything but how much each step hurts with these damn shoes scraping my bunions.

I limp to the end of the route, nonetheless, and as we head to our cars holding our signs (mine, *"Not Right America,"* with the *N-R-A* highlighted in a black box and an image of a broken-hearted kid in the upper-right corner), a guy on the street yells, "Fuck off!" when I pass him. His words land like a fist to my gut. The march up until then has been peaceful, cars whizzing by honking support, so his hostility catches me off guard. My heart stuttered in my chest.

"Sir, can I talk to you for a minute?" I ask.

He is surprisingly open to that, and we stand in front of the Eau Gallie Library, as he spits out, "You are offending five million members of the NRA with that sign."

Really? It seems a bit hyperbolic, doesn't it? But I tamp down any rising ire and say, "That's not my intention. I want to express my unhappiness with the lobbying arm of the NRA and their strident opposition to sensible gun safety measures that the majority of Americans support."

"That's not what your sign says."

I admit, rather weakly, that I can only fit so much on a poster.

He senses my weakness and moves in for the kill (he the leopard and me the baby gazelle), adamant that I am deliberately and personally offending him.

But then he asks, "What do you want?"

I tell him I want universal background checks, including at gun shows, to close loopholes, and he interrupts me—saying with great certainty that there are no such loopholes. I see immediately that he and I are stuck in the weeds, with no weed whacker in sight, so I try to shift our exchange to some little square of common ground. Surely that exists, right?

I say, "I hear you; I do. I think the issue is much more complicated than just about guns. Like why do we grow such violent men and boys? Why do they think it's a good idea to shoot up schools and movie theatres and nightclubs and concerts and churches? Why are people feeling so alienated?"

But he isn't ready to leave guns behind and says, "I have guns. I've always had guns. My sons have guns." He says the government is poised to take his guns away.

I don't know how to respond other than to say, "I don't want to take your guns away. But I can tell you that the prevalence of guns scares me. I also see that you clearly have strong feelings about this." And *that* seems to release a little bit of air out of the anger-balloon floating between us, that acknowledgment of his feelings. The energy shifts from spiky anger to something a tad softer, gentler, and sadder.

As he talks, I kept trying to place his accent. "Where are you from?" I ask.

"Zambia," he says, adding, "Once you lose rights, you never get them back."

Now, *that* is interesting. We part company after a few more minutes, amicably, no small thing given where we started. But I am rattled walking away. I wonder: Is my position unfair, too reductive? Maybe. But I also wonder about his perspective as an outsider. That part I can relate to—being the outsider. Florida often feels like a foreign country to me, given its scorching climate, fierce storms, fractious politics, strident gun advocacy, and legacy of oppression, including the disenfranchisement of over a million felons who have served their time.

And there was a certain renegade quality to the exchange that felt *so* Florida to me, after steeping myself in the local culture for thirteen years. There is a definite,

"Fuck you!" freedom of expression here, and something else too: A sense of entitlement that says, *I am going to do what I want, when I want, and you can't do anything about it*, which feels menacing—and kind of exhilarating. Just what that guy from Zambia embodied.

The Shape of Place

At home, I google Zambia and read about its history as Northern Rhodesia, its legacy of colonial racism, its natural beauty, including spectacular Victoria Falls on the border with Zimbabwe—and I wonder how much a place shapes the way we are. How is Florida shaping me? Is living here making me more courageous, more willing to step out of my comfort zone and engage with a gun-loving guy from a country on the other side of the world? Is residing among surfers—whose lifestyles (baffling to me) allow them to leave work in the middle of the day to hop on surfboards and ride the waves—making me more flexible?

I hope so.

Certainly, living in Florida invites me to look at things differently, providing lots of opportunities not to condemn others; but to try to understand them and reach common ground. For instance, while I still don't like the canines on the beach, I don't hurl invective at the owners; I just pass on by, and most days, I don't even think particularly dark thoughts about them. And there are times when I kind of get a kick out of watching their canine energy on full display—pups biting at the leash, balletic doggy leaps to snatch frisbees out of mid-air, and the obvious affection between human and beast. I can relate. Who doesn't feel restricted at times and yearn to break free? Who doesn't long for unconditional devotion? Maybe, just maybe, the dogs have something to teach me—if I can just get past that they are where I don't think they ought to be.

I imagine that some native Floridians, including my neighbors, are not thrilled with the pace of development and the state's dependence on tourism. Maybe they resent relative newbies like me and the nearly 1,000 people who move to the Sunshine State every day. Perhaps I have more in common with the dogs than I thought at first blush. Some may always view them as interlopers, but like me, they are here to stay—in Florida—home for now.

Love Cats:
Can Provide a Loving Home

Ever heard this statement: *Never make decisions when you are hungry or angry or lonely or tired*? I have, and most of the time, I even heed this sensible advice. It's easy, except for the tired part. It seems like I'm always tired these days. It's not a debilitating, all-encompassing illness-fatigue. I don't want to be misleading here. I still do most of what I want to do: write, walk, yoga, etc. But I also count my lucky stars that my glasses help hide the signs of my poor-quality sleep, the patches of dark poof under my eyes. It's not complicated. I'm tired because I just don't sleep through the night—and I awake early.

But on this particular day, I am more tired than usual. I'm just home from physically demanding training to earn the required number of credits to renew my massage therapy license. The training has left my body tired, but in a good way, and I'm looking forward to as good a night's sleep as I can get and not needing to set the alarm.

So, when I open my calendar and see I have a vet appointment tomorrow at 9 a.m., I groan.

My husband, Jim, says, "Dear, why don't you reschedule?" I, however, have been selectively and consistently ignoring his sage counsel for the duration of our marriage and "pay him no nevermind today."

So, I arise bright and early, entice our cat Cody into the carrier, grab the double-bagged pile of poo for the fecal test, and load us into the car. I set him, precious cargo, on the front seat and strap the seat belt around his case. I fiddle with the radio knob and turn up classical music to soothe the savage beast. He meows anyway. Not meek, plaintive mews, but deafening cries of protest in a range of tones heretofore unheard on this earthly plane. Did Mozart or Beethoven or Bach ever have this kind of accompaniment? Were any of them cat lovers?

At the Cat Doctor (really, that is the name of the practice), cats roam freely in the waiting area. Homer greets us. He's a friendly little guy with a stubby tail, and while he submits to my strokes, Simon lounges on the receptionist's desk, pausing in his morning ablutions to lick the receptionist's hand with sandpapery kisses. Whenever I cross the threshold into this world of cats and the good people who tend to them and their human guardians, my defenses come tumbling down, leaving a breach in my emotional wall.

In hindsight, one could see I never stood a chance when, during Cody's totally routine exam (Thank God!), Dr. B. happens to mention pet surrenders are at an all-time high, a casualty of the sputtering economy. She goes

on to say that ninety percent of these unfortunate crit-
ters are euthanized. The door to my heart, already open
a crack, creaks open a bit wider.

But, it's not just a heart thing, is it, adopting another
cat? My brain kicks in at the same second my heart opens
and compiles a list of reasons why bringing another cat
into our household is not a good idea: Introducing a new
animal into the family can be a real pain, another cat is
another expense, blah, blah. But at the same time, I can
see what I'm doing is spinning into patterned behavior,
spinning out a tiresome list of *what-ifs* that buzz around
like gnats. These fears sap my energy. (Hmm. Maybe
that's part of why I'm tired all the time.)

But there is one persistent bug I can't seem to swat
away. What if Cody, the sole cat, King Cat of the Lamb-
din/Henze household for the last three years, doesn't
cotton to the new critter? Cody definitely leans to impe-
riousness and is what my husband calls "an attention
hog." What if Cody doesn't like him or her?

So, I do what I do in times of confusion and turn to
my Tarot deck, a source of guidance that helps reach beyond my conscious awareness. I pull four cards ran-
domly from the *Osho Zen Tarot* deck. They are: **Ice-
olation**, **Guilt**, **Silence**, and **Going with the Flow**.

The first card, **Ice-olation**, symbolizes the Issue, and
shows a crying figure encased in ice. The messages to
consider: *Being too much in self, tears heal, and love and
warmth dissolve boundaries.* The second card, **Guilt**, symbolizes an Internal Influence I may not be aware of. **Guilt**
depicts a distraught figure, mouth open in a scream, a

skinny, wrinkly, disembodied monster, hands clawing at its head. The messages: *You, reader, may be caught up in a cycle of despair and hopelessness.* The third card, the External Influence, is **Silence**: A full moon hangs like a third eye in the middle of a huge head in a starry sky. It whispers, *Come home to yourself; there is nothing to do, nowhere to go.* Finally, the fourth card symbolizes the Resolution. It is, **Going with the Flow**, in which a lone figure swims in a blue sea. It says, *Trust and relax; you can float now.* It's in the cards, isn't it? It's all here: tears and fears, silence and flow, trust. Sounds about right. I allow the reading to wash over my soul.

Six days later, Jim and I drive to a local pet-adoption event. We fill out the application for adoption, which says it is designed to help place the animal with the most suitable family. We answer a multitude of questions, including:

Q: How many hours a day will the pet be alone?

A: It varies, two–six hours.

Q: Will the pet be permitted on the furniture?

A: Yes.

Q: Do you or anyone in your family have allergies to hair or dust?

A: No.

Q: Are you aware of the yearly costs of pet ownership?

A: Yes.

Q: Vet care can total in the hundreds or even thousands of dollars for extensive health issues. Are you prepared to meet these requirements?

A: Yes.

Q: Have you ever surrendered an animal to a shelter?
A: No.
Q: What was the disposition of your previous animals?
If euthanized, why?
A: Euthanized geriatric cats at ages fifteen and sixteen,
with debilitating health problems and pain.
Q: How long were these animals part of your family?
A: Fifteen years, sixteen years.

And this one, about twenty-six questions in, which I would have put first:

Q: Why do you want this pet?
A: We love cats, want a companion for Cody-cat, we
can provide a loving home.

Within minutes of completing the two-page questionnaire, we are drawn by an invisible but powerful force to a cage that holds a seven-pound, seven-month-old, gray-and-black tabby with green eyes who lets us hold him and fawn over him. We now at that moment this is the cat for us. We name him Cayce, after Edgar Cayce, the sleeping prophet and psychic of Virginia Beach: no lofty expectations here. We do not learn until a few days later that Cayce is a ground cat and doesn't much care for being picked up, and that he has a most active tail that twitches at the slightest sweet word from us. But, on that day, he lets us hold him to our heart's content. Surely, Cody, too, will find him the cat's meow.

Wrong! Crabby Cody does not cede the mastery of his domain willingly. He dislikes the interloper. He is all growls and arched back, and hisses. While we understand his behavior, we are still dumbstruck by the range of noises that a puny, ten-pound bag of fur can emit. Where are these guttural growls and spiky hisses coming from? Where is our sweet, lovable pile of fur, who butts our hands for scritches of his ears and lolls on our laps, rolling onto his back so we can stroke the length of his spotted belly? Where is that animal who calmly lies at our feet while we read the paper at the dining room table?

Cayce does not help his case. Although I watched his foster mother dose him with flea medicine before we left the adoption event, fleas torment him. When he sits on me one night while we watch TV, fleas crawl over his handsome face. We up the flea treatment, but he still scratches incessantly and leaves symmetrical bald spots on his ears and patches of skin exposed on his neck. His sensitive intestinal tract delivers poo that gives new meaning to the word pungent. We are grateful that we have a garage to house the cat boxes.

In these early days of adjustment with a flea-bitten, stinky defecator, Jim sleeps his customary sleep of the dead, while I lie awake wide-eyed, spinning out worst-case scenarios. In the netherworld, as I twitch in between sleeping and waking, I imagine us all outfitted in gas masks, tiny little custom-made ones for the cats, all of us lost in a fog of insecticide. Sleep, when it comes, provokes uneasy, repetitive dreams of cat boxes overflowing with malodorous poo and cats slicing at one another with razor-sharp claws.

Yet, once again, the worst never comes to pass in the real world outside my head. In a few weeks, the cats make their peace. One day, Cody just stopped with the hissing, the growls, the disdainful sniffs. Why did that happen? Not a clue, although I think it has to do with the chemistry between the two of them. Cody has always been a sniffer, often stopping in his tracks to raise his head, wiggle his nose, and take in the quality of the air around him. He sniffs Cayce a lot, never backs up, never recoils in horror. I think he likes the way Cayce smells. I know I do when I bury my face in his fur and take a deep inhale.

And they are complementary cats: Cody is jumpy and sensitive; Cayce is calm and serene. Cay's *Whatever, dude* vibe casts a calming spell, not just over Cody, but over the entire household. And, come to think of it, Cody and Cayce kind of mirror their human companions: It's probably obvious that I am Cody, and Jim is Cayce.

I am able, finally, to join my husband in slumber—but only until dawn breaks. Then, the cats, best buddies now, alert and rarin' to go, tumble through the house chasing each other, waking me too early with the sounds of their kittycat fleet-feet, making sufficient restful sleep still an elusive commodity for me. But that seems a small price to pay for a fuller house.

Reading Mary Oliver at 4:30 a.m.

Recently, I have been reading Mary Oliver's collection of poems *Blue Horses* at 4:30 in the morning. I'm up reading because I have a miserable toothache that makes sleep elusive, if not impossible. However, even with an achy jaw, Mary Oliver is good company at this hushed hour of a new day when the rest of our household still sleeps.

The Unitarians initially turned me on to Mary Oliver. I had stumbled over the threshold of River Road Unitarian Church (RRUC) in Bethesda, Maryland, one Sunday morning in the mid-eighties, after a friend, who also grew up in another denomination, told me she found it welcoming and a good fit. This was during a particularly low time in my life. I had trouble articulating specifically what was wrong with me back then. Still, I knew it had a lot to do with trying *really* hard—for a *really* long time—to act and be okay despite decades of untreated anxiety and depression, which were always waiting patiently offstage in the wings, threatening to pull me under.

I looked okay on the outside—except for my teeth cracking from excessive grinding during the night. Inside, however, I could never fully shake a feeling of unease, an inability to relax, always hypervigilant, stretched taut like a rubber band past capacity, waiting to snap. I was desperate for relief and, as Marianne Williamson likes to say, "Desperate people do desperate things." Fortunately, *desperate* for me did not mean using firearms or heavy drugs, but instead finding a new church home.

Immediately, I knew RRUC was the place for me. During one of those early Sunday services, the minister read Mary Oliver's poem "Wild Geese." Listening, I knew Mary, too, was for me. In that poem, she writes about despair and repentance, the steadfastness of nature, and about wild geese heading home, announcing their place in the "family of things." When the reverend read the poem, I felt something I hadn't felt in a very long time. It was hope—and that maybe there was a place for me, too, in the family of things.

It was abundantly clear to me that Oliver knew from firsthand experience what she was writing about—depths and heights and a way to go on, drawing sustenance from eternal, unchanging verities. Whether it was true or not, I came to believe that that poem, that day, Mary Oliver helped set me back on a track that renewed my desire to go on living.

And I did go on living, obviously, and now I am often awake at 4:30 a.m., thanks not only, like tonight, to a toothache, but to a chronic urgency to pee. Each night, I toss aside the covers and quick-step it across the room to the bathroom, clutching my privates so I don't leak urine along the way. The leakage is worse since a laser procedure a little over a year ago that was supposed to help with both the frequency and urgency. At the appointment, the doc was hesitant, tentative, before she stuck the wand up my lady parts, looking to the technician for guidance. Her uncertainty did not boost my confidence.

That first night at home after the procedure, I watched TV with my husband, Jim, as is our routine. During either *The Daily Show*, or *The Good Wife*, or *The Strain* (the latter an unusual pick for us if you look at our viewing history since we are not generally big on zombies), I pause the DVR to dart across the hall to the bathroom. Numb, I cannot feel the urine dribble out, and I think, *Oh, my God. I'm worse since this $750 elective procedure, which is not covered by insurance or our Flexible Spending Account.*

At the initial evaluation and before the procedure, the doctor told me I would likely improve with one treatment, but of course, she could not make any guarantees. At my follow-up visit, the very first thing she said was, "Would you like to repeat the procedure?" She did not ask how I was or how I felt, which left me declining her offer—even managing to do so in a civil tone.

There were signs that this was not the practice for me. I don't always ignore my intuition, my internal guidance. But I did this time. Why? Why did I ignore my gut feeling that this was not a great fit for me? I was desperate—again. I was desperate for help to relieve my urgent and frequent urination—and that is the practice's specialty. I was starting to curtail my activities because of my pee problem, and all conventional wisdom recommends seeking help when daily activities are impaired. I was hoping they could help me.

At my first appointment, during sign-in, the TV blaring in the background made it hard to hear the receptionist, and I suggested to her it might be helpful to turn the TV down or even mute it. Without looking up, she said, "The TV stays on." I did not miss the hostile chill in her voice.

What I wanted to do at that moment was get a baseball bat and smash the screen and its perpetual loop of bad news, which is hardly conducive to healing. I could have just turned around and walked out the door. But what I did instead was take a seat across the room as far away from the TV as I could get like a good little sheep. *Baaaa!*

When I left that first appointment, I almost did not recognize my little Mazda Miata baking in the sun in the treeless parking lot. When I went in, my car was shiny metallic blue, bright and sparkly and clean, but when I returned to it, the car was completely splattered with white bird shit. It must have been a mega flock that flew overhead and, with some weird bird synchronization, let loose at just the right/wrong moment over the target below, my car.

At the next appointment, I followed directions and arrived with a full bladder. An assistant promptly took me back into the bowels of the operation to a room, where she told me to sit on a "special commode." I draped a flimsy piece of paper across my nether regions while a technician, a brusque, tough woman with stiff hair and an air of constant aggrievement, administered the urodynamic study to assess how well my urinary system works. She inserted catheters into my urethra and vagina and then took her seat and fiddled with dials that drove in water—ramping up the pressure until I could not stand it another second and let go. A torrent of pee hit the pot with a splish-splash while I eeked out involuntary utterances of profound relief. She calmly tracked my level of bladder tolerance and retention.

There is a certain intimacy to the process, and I kind of admired her matter-of-factness, her unflappability, and her obvious level of skill. But that sense of intimacy loosened her tongue to utter appalling remarks about why blacks and whites have no business mixing. She actually said that: "Blacks and whites have no business mixing."

I sat there, a grown woman suspended over a portable potty, undergoing the intimate process. I didn't speak up, and I felt like a coward as she turned the dial on the instrument of torture. I liken her to the sadistic Nazi played by Laurence Olivier in *The Marathon Man*, and I was the hapless patient, played by Dustin Hoffman.

However, he had it much, much worse, with a dental drill pounding on his sore tooth.

Loose Lips went on to tell me she had been "let go" from a previous job with no explanation and was still completely baffled by this injustice. I felt lousy for not speaking up. What I wanted to say was something like this: *Shut the hell up! Keep your racist remarks to yourself!* Or maybe something a bit less inflammatory: *You clearly have strong feelings about this. I have strong feelings, too, that are very different from yours, and I find your comments off-putting. Let's talk about something else.*

But I stayed mute and withdrew into my little cowardly cocoon. Nausea gripped my guts, and I broke out in a cold, clammy sweat, teetering on the edge of a major anxiety attack with my heart pounding away in my chest while I perched on that special commode.

And yet ... and yet ... I returned to that practice three more times. The first time, I got the results of the test, which the doc skimmed over to push medication and the new laser procedure. The second time, I underwent the new laser procedure. And the third time, the doctor mumbled a sentence or two, which turned out to be the entirety of the follow-up to the laser procedure. Previously, I had been told that this third appointment was just a routine follow-up, and would be included in the self-funded, non-insurance-covered, non-FSA-covered $750 fee. However, this doctor's office billed my insurance company a gasp-inducing $200 for the five-minute appointment. I protested when I got the Explanation of

Benefits in the mail, and they told me this: "We can't undo what we did with your insurance company."

I could, however, undo my next appointment, which I did, never to return.

A year later, I had a toothache that started on a Tuesday afternoon in my lower jaw on the right side, and despite wishing and hoping, it did not go away in a day or two, and instead led to root canal treatment a week later. Unfortunately, the roots were calcified, probably from chronic inflammation, the endodontist said, which required the insertion of chemicals into the canal and then giving them a month to break up the blockages before proceeding.

I asked, "Can't you just blast the damn thing?" He looked at me as if I were the endodontically challenged dolt I am and said, with equal parts incredulity and compassion, "No, that would fracture your tooth, and we want to do everything we can to save your tooth."

A month later, I am on a second round of antibiotics to address the searing, throbbing, aching pain that snakes up my head and bursts into a full-blown migraine every other day. Some days, I contemplate sticking my head in the oven. I don't have any kids to make sure are out of the house before I turn the gas on, à la Sylvia Plath, but I do have three cats that I do not want to kill, and I can't put them outside because they never go out, and I don't know if they'd survive. And besides, my death would upset my elderly father, and there are so many good books yet to read that I think I'll stay around a bit longer. Maybe, I'll even stay around a long, long, long time, like my two great-aunts, who lived to be over one hundred—although that doesn't seem like such an accomplishment now that I'm in my sixties.

Instead, I once again follow a doctor's orders and take the second round of antibiotics as prescribed: two every six hours for the first twenty-four, and then one every six hours until they're gone. I set the alarm for 4:30 in the morning—in case my urge to pee doesn't wake me in time—to swallow the pill at the appointed interval with generous amounts of water, and I don't lie down for ten minutes after taking it because that's what the directions on the bottle warn against doing. Instead, I prop myself up to sitting. I blink, blink, and blink again, trying to moisturize my dry, scratchy eyes as I pick up the book on the stand next to the bed, *Blue Horses*, by Mary Oliver, and crack it open while I wait for the medicine to kick in.

Wind

The wind wakes me this morning, scraping palm fronds across the air-conditioner unit stuck in the window. The wind wakes me this morning, together with an urgency to pee that I cannot ignore. I trot to the bathroom, take care of business, and then pull on the pajama bottoms I've kicked off in the middle of the night, now lying in a blue-and-white heap of flannel beside the bed.

Too hot, too cold, too hot, too cold, just right. Too hot, too cold, too hot, too cold, just right. I feel like a grown-up version of Goldilocks, but rather than sampling porridges and chairs, I kick off pajama bottoms and yank off sheets and blankets all through the night, desperate to find the combo that is just right. Does this roller coaster ride on the ups and downs of my internal thermostat ever end?

It's been one, two, three, four ... seven-plus years since my last period, which turns out to be one of those lasts I didn't know was going to be a last. Boxes of tampons and maxi pads still sit half-full in the bathroom cabinet, gathering dust. I don't miss having periods.

But I do miss my mother. One day, while I sit in my mother's living room, she looks at me quizzically and asks, "Who are you?" It'd be an excellent question, or at least a provocative conversation starter, an existentialist exploration, in any other context than this one, in which my courteous, well-mannered mother is losing her mind. Alzheimer's disease is relentless in its pursuit of my mother. She trips and falls and fails to outrun the beast nipping at her heels. Alzheimer's is kind of like the Law pursuing Bonnie and Clyde and Butch and the Sundance Kid. But they were criminals, while the only crime my mother ever committed was growing old.

Just like that, at a snap of my fingers, I get refiled from only daughter to some middle-aged woman with dirty-blonde hair who visits from time to time. I do miss my mother—or, more accurately, I miss the mother who knows who I am.

This early morning in Florida, I take out my earplugs and place them on a tissue to use again. I turn off the sound machine and pull the curtain aside on the door to the patio to watch the wind whip through the trees, bending them to kiss the ground. The large, gray tarp we covered the patio furniture with a year ago, while the house was painted, has blown up against the door and will require a good shove with *oomph* to push it out of the way.

I pad upstairs, quiet as a mouse, footsteps muffled by my husband's white gym socks. He has been up for hours, much earlier to bed, and much earlier to rise than I. He sits at the computer and grunts a greeting without looking up, while at the same time, two cats lounge on the bed behind him, Cody on Jim's backpack, tawny gold against black, Cayce atop a pile of freshly folded clothes, gray and black against gray and black. Jim will slip on these clean clothes in a couple of hours after he sweats through the black shorts and stained white T-shirt he'll wear during his rigorous bike ride along the river. He will make sure to tie a bandana around his head to catch the copious volume of sweat he drips that otherwise would slide down his broad forehead and sting his eyes. Fierce wind or not, Jim is a champion sweater.

Both cats seek the rays of sun streaming in through the paw-smeared windows. Cayce, a fat gray-and-black tabby that the vet wants to lose weight (she says she'd like to see more of his waist), rolls over, and I bend to smoosh my face into his white jelly-belly and breathe him in deeply. He tolerates this for a few seconds before he bites my hair and rolls away. I wonder where Catsby is, but then I hear crunching in the bathroom and know he is eating breakfast.

Gusts whoosh. Trees bend. Palm fronds strike the house and litter the lawn and driveway. The wind whistles down the fireplace. The broken damper clangs. A long, thin piece of hard plastic breaks free from the window frame and slaps the house and window. It is not an easy fix, this window two stories up. Jim will have to break out the tall ladder slung along the side of the wall in the garage that is pure hell to maneuver through doorways. It'd be easier just to open the garage door, but then we'd have to wrangle cats, counting one, two, three to make sure they are all accounted for and don't make a break for it, running willy-nilly out in the yard, which is forbidden territory. Although, I can't imagine they'd go far, especially in this wind.

Jim will likely swear when he heaves the ungainly ladder up and out the front door, although he's not really a cursing kind of guy. As a last resort, he may even ask for my help. "Dear, can you help me with ...?" I will drop whatever I am doing to assist him and take orders from him for a few minutes, something I am not particularly good at doing.

The plastic tapping against the window drives me nuts. Jim knows that, although I will try not to, I will complain about it until he fixes it, even though I don't want him climbing a long ladder set at a precarious angle against a white stucco house in a strong wind.

We get on each other's nerves. How could we not, after twenty-three years together? He is neat, and I am messy. He is patient, and I am impatient. He is taciturn, and I am volatile. He sweats, and I barely perspire. He forgets, and I remember all kinds of transgressions that would better be forgotten.

But whenever we part when travelling, we play a little game. The one left behind says, "What are you going to tell the pilot?" The one leaving says, "Precious cargo." Although sometimes I can't resist saying, "Crash and burn," which, of course, I don't mean. I'm just trying to be amusing. I cling to him in those final seconds before we part and smoosh my face into his chest and inhale his scent until he, like Cayce, has had enough and pulls away. Our devotion to each other rivals what we feel for our cats. High praise, indeed!

It is 2:30 now, and the afternoon is bright and sunny. The marsh grasses bend sideways in gusts that near fifty mph, according to the weatherman on the local news. He is a handsome man with gel in his hair, who always wears such a nice suit to accompany the smirky smile we never tire speculating about. A lone heron stands on the bank of the pond, unperturbed and undisturbed, its magnificent wings spread wide to dry its feathers in the turbocharged wind. Any minute now, any minute, this tall, gray bird will fold those beauties down, then raise them up again, and soar off into the wind.

The Acupuncturist and the Woman

"**C**hange!" the diminutive acupuncturist barks at me. At that moment, I suspect she does not mean merely change my clothes into the gown she's offering, but, rather, change my entire personality.

This is our first session, and I am a bit taken aback by her directness. She comes highly recommended, however, by my long-term hairstylist, a generous woman with Rubenesque curves and dark, cascading hair, who not only manages to make my stick-straight hair look good, but who also shares my interest in complementary health. She spoke highly of Dr. W., telling me she is more than just your average acupuncturist; she's as much a healer, not only clearing energetic blocks and imbalances, but often sharing insights about the blocks she finds. I find this enormously appealing and a natural complement to the six years of energy-healing studies I recently finished in Miami. But I feel a tad nervous, too, imagining the vulnerability of exposing myself to some-one purported to "see" beneath the surface.

Dr. W. and I square off across the healing table, she on her padded, spinning stool and me on a hard, metal chair. A look of concern clouds her delicate features as she turns a letter-size file folder labeled *Lambdin, Beth* lengthwise. "Here's your husband's love for you," she says, dragging the pen across the top to inch eleven, the full length of the manila folder.

I feel a little uneasy. I was not expecting Jim would be part of my session.

Then she declares, "Here's your love for your hus-band." I sit ramrod straight, holding my breath as her pen skims the file folder a second time. Like trying to bend spoons with my mind, I focus on her hand, willing it to move the pen all the way to the edge of the file folder, so it matches Jim's love for me. Instead, she stops around inch four—seven inches short of Jim's full-folder line. My breath tumbles out of me, and I collapse in the chair, shoulders hunched.

She sets down the pen and stares at me, all calm and Zen-like.

I feel blindsided. All I hear is: *Your love for Jim is a third of his love for you. You are a terrible wife and a horri-ble person.* And the door on my stingy little heart slams shut.

I want to mutter a bunch of defensive excuses on my behalf and contrast them eloquently with a litany of Jim's faults. But I shut up and allow this odd, unexpected exchange to settle between us for a few moments. Then

I say, "Yes, there's no doubt he is much more tolerant and patient than I am."

She nods her head like the wise woman she may be and agrees. While I forget her exact words, she implies we would not be together if he weren't such a good man.

Wow! All color drains from the room, turning it a stark black and white.

I feel like total crap and get busy taking my lousy-wife inventory. Here is a sampling of how I criticize the most important person in my life: what and how much he eats (delivered under the guise of being concerned about his health); his incessant throat clearing (especially bad in the first hour after he consumes too much of his poor food choices); and his weight gains and losses. He gets the brunt of my complaining, often about things that are totally out of his control, a mix of the low-, medium-, and high-level cacophony of life in the modern world, which I find an affront to my delicate senses and subsequently whip up into a toxic brew.

Suddenly, I see Jim swept away in a tsunami of my negativity. I feel ashamed of my petty, small self that finds it necessary to try to shrink him to my size. No wonder he craves those sweet, over-sized cookies from the local co-op; he isn't getting much sweetness from me.

Then I compile the sainted-husband inventory: his willingness to watch documentary films with me (true, he falls asleep but snorts awake with a willing spirit); his unwavering support as I've changed careers not once or twice, but three times, all with considerable expense and retraining, each time with a significant cut in pay, and never once a word of complaint (other than a joke now and then that he'll retire when I write that bestseller); and his ability to set aside his fatigue to listen to the trivia of my day when he arrives home from work.

Could this be the good doc's plan, to make me feel like shit? Is she invoking a version of tough love to deliberately make me feel lousy? Even in my addled, shamed state, I doubt that. I am just another patient looking for something I haven't found—yet. And since I waited over a month for this appointment, I want to get as much out of it as possible. Demonizing the messenger is not a good plan.

This acupuncturist, adept at reading the body and its plethora of not-so-subtle cues, is just jiggling the key in the lock of the door to the basement, where I've tossed some stinky garbage. She is merely a catalyst.

She studies my intake form and probes my litany of complaints: my intermittent abdominal pain, my teeth grinding, my back and neck aches, and my lousy sleep, frequently interrupted by an urgency to urinate. She says anger is wreaking havoc with my body—and not with her voice rising at the end of the sentence—leaving room for it to be a question, but with a drop in her inflection as if stating the obvious. I find that really annoying, her certainty. But I just sit with her words and feel the anger and its wear and tear on my body.

Her words are hard to hear. They are also kind of a relief to hear. I let her words sink in.

She goes on to say that Jim and I often play out the male and female roles in reverse, and she doesn't make it sound like it's a good thing. As she speaks, I consider the many ways I have been rewarded for my hard-driving, persistent personality, especially at work, and I also see how those same traits can make a marriage challenging. Jim has said on more than one occasion, "You try to control the uncontrollable." Was I willing to give that up? Was surrender even in my repertoire?

Beyond gender roles and human limitations, the truth, or as close as I can come to it, is this: I am tired of being me in the same old, habitual ways. I long to rest in the comfort of the secure relationship Jim and I have built together over more than twenty years. I long to rest in the arms of this good man. I long to treat him more kindly and more like the excellent life partner that he is.

And I realize that, no matter how wise the acupuncturist may be, her picture of us is incomplete. It's not like Jim is some passive wimp. He's worried me on more than one occasion when he arrives home from roller skating and recounts how he's pounded on the hoods of cars of inconsiderate motorists who have cut him off and nearly run him down. And there is the infamous movie-theatre incident from early in our relationship when he showered a woman with a mouthful of soda after she told me to go "fuck myself" when I asked her to stop talking during the film. An ex-wife incident floats back into my consciousness, too. In response to her criticism about what he was wearing to her son's college graduation, Jim tore off his tie and ripped off his shirt, buttons flying with enough velocity to put an eye out. At least I haven't criticized his clothing choices, I rationalize. But that's not entirely true. He is sartorially challenged (in my opinion), and I have asked him to please not wear his "hobo" clothes when we go out in public.

Jim and I both have fuses; mine is just shorter, and his is longer. We have set points in our personalities. He leans towards impassive stoicism; I lean towards active martyrdom. But we are also mutable. While I complain too much, I also rail against injustice and spring into action. Jim may be slow to rile, but he can also be slow to act. He once said life with me is never dull.

I know Jim sometimes hides candy from me. I have never looked for it and wouldn't violate his privacy. However, I do accidentally surprise him sometimes when he sits at the computer. He doesn't hear me coming, and when I lean in to kiss him, I smell chocolate on his breath. "Where is it?" I ask, and he laughs but never tells me. Maybe he hides a stash of kindness next to his stash of candy. Perhaps I can start my own collection of treats and kindness and compassion and draw upon it as needed.

Shades of gray return to the acupuncture room as I lie on the table with needles stuck in my head and my left hand with a blanket draped over my lower body to chase away the chill. My new, truth-telling doc orders me to lie still and not move my hand. She asks me to think about a specific incident that makes me angry. Easy—big, strange, unleashed dogs on the beach bound into my awareness, and I bear down with all my considerable powers of obsession. The clock ticks on the wall. I hear her exhale and feel something subtly shift in me, as if she is pouring a drain cleaner through my meridians, flushing away years of emotional debris. She repeats the process several times. She tells me to keep "emptying out," and, over time, a sense of peace replaces the old stuck anger and shame. At the end of the session, she asks me how I feel. I say, "I feel like I'm floating on the ceiling of the Sistine Chapel." Not only does everything feel right in the larger world—everything feels right in Beth's world.

I leave the appointment deeply relaxed and deeply disturbed—but in a good way. On the drive home, I want to feel bad about myself, to scratch that itch about all the ways I fall short of being the perfect partner. But my heart isn't in it. Like my computer, after a successful reboot, my hardware is unchanged, but my software, my soft, tender insides, have a new set point. But I also know a one-shot deal will unlikely be enough for me to maintain this new set point. More visits lie ahead.

That night after work, Jim kneels on the bathroom floor on his creaky, surgically improved knees to pick up cat-food crumbles and crush the tiny ants that seek the cats' water. Our chubby middle cat, Cayce, arches his back and brushes up against Jim as he tends to his needs. My heart swells with love as I watch this tableau. I take stock of how this man tends to my needs, too, often not with words but with considerate deeds and unwavering support.

We leave on vacation the next day, which gives me lots of opportunities to be a softer, gentler version of me. Instead of complaining about the inconveniences that accompany travel, I notice how kind people are. The hotel staff upgrades us to an executive suite. The breakfast lady with the lilting Jamaican accent expertly flips perfect omelets and bids us a good day. The friendly trolley driver insists we hold up for several minutes at the last stop. Then she pulls the lever, and the trolley door screeches open so we can better hear the street busker, a woman with a swelling, pregnant belly singing an operatic aria. Jim leans forward in the front seat and contorts his body to look out the open door.

Behind him, I can't see over or around his head for a moment. A flash of anger leaps out of me—but instead of grasping for it, I let it go. I focus instead on what's right in front of me: glorious music from a pregnant lady on the sidewalk and my husband with tears streaking his face. As the woman concludes her aria on this sunny afternoon, the driver pulls the lever to shut the door, just as the door to my heart creaks open. I'm not sure that this is the kind of change the acupuncturist has in mind, but it's a good start.

The Beths

"I'm sorry. I don't recognize you," says the woman in the parking lot of the Cocoa Beach Library when I greet her with a hearty, "Hello."

For some bizarre reason, embarrassment grips *me*, and like an aging ballerina, slightly off-balance, I twirl around tossing my ponytail. "Maybe, it's my hair. I have my hair back today."

But it's not the hair; I see from her quizzical look that she just doesn't remember me.

How can that be? Tiny little gremlins of hurt ding my heart. While we are not close friends (obviously), we inhale the same stale library air for a couple of hours every week in a local writing group. Each week, some complement of us lays bare our souls on top of the conference room table. We expose our works in progress. We open ourselves up to the scrutiny of others, who offer critique and occasional praise that, yes, indeed, we are on the right track—or at least a relatable track.

Am I really that forgettable? I don't think so. On the charisma scale, I put myself about in the middle. No question, I do not generate a golden glow like Emma Thompson or Emma Stone or Barack Obama when he gives one of his room-rocking oratories, but you can tell the difference between the woodwork and me. I am not a quiet, meek mouse-lady, even if I am in that demographic that advertisers no longer target.

Why is it that some people make an impression—indelible and long-lasting—like the stain on that favorite blouse I can't get out despite my best efforts, even using bleach? Why is it that some of us stick in others' memories, and some of us barely register?

This question drives me to self-absorption and distraction—and ultimately, to Google. I type in *Beth Lambdin,* and in 0.12 seconds, 57,000 entries appear. I am amazed at how many of us there are. So much for being terminally unique.

A sampling of internet Beth Lambdins follows:

Beth #1, the Humanitarian Beth, works at the Michael J. Fox Foundation in New York City and funds grant applications for Parkinson's research.

Beth #2, from Plano, Texas, is a motorcycle fanatic interested in starting a new Harley-Davidson Meetup group. She and her husband are the proud owners of a 2004 Road King Classic and an 883 Sportster.

Beth #3 is part of a hypothetical problem that students from The University of Maryland School of Law Moot Court Board created. In their scenario, this Beth is the last person to see her neighbor, Carol Lynn Stuart, a twenty-six-year-old mother of two young children, alive after a screaming match with her abusive husband.

Beth #4 is the mother of an ardent young Republican, her eleven-year-old daughter, who says that her family's pro-life values are the lens through which she judges all political candidates. Her daughter holds the distinction as the youngest member of the San Joaquin County Republican Women's Club.

Beth #5 is a teenage soccer superstar combining skill and toughness with athletic prowess.

In Stockton, California, Beth #6 *"Closes her eyes and raises her hands heavenward in the noontime sunshine at Dean De Carli Waterfront Square as she prays with more than 100 people gathered to celebrate the National Day of Prayer."*

As for me, this same Google search shows I am a lover of words, a member of a Unitarian Universalist book group discussing Annie Dillard's *Pilgrim at Tinker Creek*, and a freelance writer who frequently writes about film.

What would it be like to round up all these different Beths? Would we stand together in awkward silence and strain to find common ground beyond our shared name? Or would we form some giant, multi-faceted gem that sparkles with the brilliance of a thousand suns? Could I resist the temptation to judge these other Beths by the tiny amount of information I've gleaned about them from the internet? Or could I lay aside my prejudices about politics and lifestyle to embrace these women (and girls) in their uniqueness and complexity? Could they do the same with me? With a nod to Ralph Ellison, would any of them share my moment of feeling like an invisible woman? And what reflections of myself would I see in the mirrors they raised?

I consider each one.

Have I been a humanitarian contributing to the welfare of others beyond my self-centered self-interests, like Beth #1? My first reaction: I'm no Mother Teresa, but few are. I've been a teacher, and if there's ever a profession that ought to be considered for sainthood, that'd be it. I did my best to connect with a whole range of kids along a broad intellectual-emotional-social-ethnic-cultural-economic spectrum, and to bathe them in respect and transmit my love of learning. Often, tangible results were elusive, but I learned too that you never know what kind of impact you have. You never know what sinks in and makes a difference over the long haul. One of my cherished mementos is a card from a college student with dyslexia I tutored during his four years at The George Washington University in Washington, D.C. He wrote at graduation, "You helped me to be not just a better student, but a better human being."

On to Beth #2. Can I substitute a scooter for the motorcycle? As a nervous bride on my honeymoon in Bermuda, I clung to my husband, full of anxiety and severely disoriented, as we sped around on the opposite side of the road from how we drive in the United States. But maybe it's not about the type of conveyance. Maybe the message from Motorcycle Beth is about pushing beyond self-imposed limits. Have I swung on a trapeze without a net? Well, no, but I did walk sixty miles in three days on bloody, blistered feet, over hill and dale, through suffocating heat, to raise money for breast cancer research and awareness. The majority of my donations ranged from $25–$100, for which I was grateful, but one student's mother stunned me when she donated $500 to my efforts. Aren't people something?

What about moot-court witness Beth #3? Thankfully, no one in my immediate sphere has ever been murdered, but I know the agony of sudden loss. A best friend died unexpectedly after open-heart surgery; a beloved cousin drowned in a freak accident; an ex-boyfriend took his own life. These are losses that blasted away pieces of my heart that I fear are lost for good.

What about maternal Beth #4 with the politically active young daughter? I've never been a mother to human children, which brings both regret and relief. But don't we all nurture and support our family, friends, co-workers, and animal companions? I'd take a bullet for our cats. Well, that's a bit hyperbolic, but I love them with a ferocity that borders on the deranged. When I told a friend recently that the vet wants to take our oldest cat's eye out since it may be cancerous and that we are seriously considering doing it, she said, "You sure do love your cats." This is undeniably true.

And athletic Beth #5? A disastrous softball team try-out as a teen leaves me scarred for life, and I use the experience to feed a belief that I'm not athletic. But is that true? I am a formidable ping-pong player, and when in that zone, I move with fluidity and grace.

Finally, there's devotee Beth #6. This one is easy if it's about spirituality rather than merely religion. It's unlikely that you'll find me communing with God in the public square. However, I pray and meditate privately and consistently and have faith that all prayers matter and that all people possess a basic core goodness (at least that's the aspiration).

Beyond these connections, I suspect that, generally, all of us Beths are more alike than first blush would indicate. Aren't we *all* more alike than different? At some level, don't we all want the same things: to be loved, to love, to contribute to the world, to be heard, and to feel like we matter? I am grateful to my internet Beths for reflecting parts of myself I do not always see. I am thankful to my Beths for shushing the voices that whisper, "You are invisible."

But while the Beths may mirror some parts of myself, aspects I would probably benefit from by acknowledging more fully, I trust there is a holy whole that is uniquely mine. I wish I could open up the *Book of Beth Lambdin* and study that blueprint. However, I suspect I've been given glimpses of it through dreams and beach-walk reveries and those "knowings" (like a vision I had of marrying Jim while on our first date strolling around the reflecting pool in front of the U.S. Capitol) that swim into my consciousness when I sleep or shift out of my habitual, perpetual busyness. I suspect, too, that more will be revealed as I age—at least I hope so.

I know I want to be of this world, but not *too* much of this world, with its oft-dualistic black-and-white thinking and fractiousness and focus on the negative. I believe that I am on a trajectory to realize my uniqueness, including my complexity and contradictions, more fully *and* to appreciate (and value) how I am just like everyone else. Ultimately, perhaps it's about finding comfort living with the paradoxes that make up daily life on this plane.

Which is where I am now—on this earthly plane. And who knows? Maybe there's a Harley in my future, one I'll hop aboard, rev up, and ride roaring out of the shadows of doubt.

I bet the lady from my writing group would remember that.

My Mother's Ring

You know that nagging feeling you get that there's something significant about a day, but you just can't put your finger on what it is? That's how I felt this past Sunday—and it threw me off balance and gave me the dropsies. My cereal spoon clanged to the floor on its way to my bowl, and my delicate, gold, filigree earring (half of a favorite pair I inherited from my mother-in-law) rolled under the bureau on its way to my ear lobe.

Just what was it I couldn't remember?

This fuzzy-headedness is not uncommon. While it's not an everyday occurrence by any means, just last week, I read a *New Yorker* article at bedtime and couldn't remember what it was about the very next day. I *do* remember the article about the Los Angeles mountain lions and the lengths we are willing to go to, including building a kind of High Line for them. The goal is for the cats to expand their territories, which are currently encroached on by developments, and provide a safe way for them to cross the busy freeways without getting smooshed by cars (hence, the elevated wildlife overpass). The hope is that this safe passage will give them a better chance to mate out of their family and diversify their gene pool and not go extinct in a few decades. Now, as if right on cue, Cody, our exceedingly handsome domestic cat, with a tawny coat not unlike that of his wilder cousins, winds around my legs and then whines at the door to go out on the porch.

But back to my fuzzy-headedness two days ago. At about 9:40 a.m., on that Sunday morning in late February, which was warm and so overcast that when I dashed out to catch the launch when the sonic boom shook the house, I could not see it through the soft, gray blanket the clouds had thrown over the sky.

I had a meeting to get to, so I pulled on new yoga pants and a long top I think marketers call *raspberry*. I threw on a long, gray cardigan and gray Keds. The sweater was too much weight, but exposing my upper arms in public feels like an affront to nature, so I sweat instead. So much for embracing aging gracefully.

About 10 a.m., I exchanged pleasantries with a woman I know—not well, but well enough to hug her and mean it. She said she was fine when I asked, but I later heard her say, "My sister died unexpectedly on Valentine's Day." Before I left, I offered her my condolences. She told me her sister had Parkinson's, but her death was unexpected, and that she is sad, but okay. She is not a woman who likes the focus on her, and there was a pregnant pause between us. Instead of allowing it, respecting the silence, and despite knowing better on some intuitive level, I launched into a story about how after my mother died, right before the memorial service, I opened the heavy, rental-car door into my lip—leaving it bloody, swollen, and painful to the touch. I then dabbed at it with a tissue all through her service, including during the prepared remarks I made about our relationship, taking care not to drip blood on my fitted, black sheath. It was one of those stories I wanted to stop as soon as I started, but I couldn't figure out how to extricate myself gracefully, so I finished it—keeping it mercifully short. My friend smiled indulgently.

As I drove home, a jolt ran through my body: That day, February 19, 2017, was the sixth anniversary of my mother's death. Oh, my gosh, how did I not remember that? I remembered so clearly the day six years before, February 19, 2011, a frigid upstate New York day, with slippery, snow-slicked roads and flurries dancing in the sky. Late in the afternoon, after a weak sun called it quits for the day, my sister-in-law Claudia and I grasped hands and prayed my mother off to wherever the dying go when they leave this earthly plane. Claudia let out an involuntary yelp, tinged with ecstasy (maybe glimpsing the hereafter?). At the same time, a sharp jolt rocketed through my body—not unlike the jolt I felt today when I remembered I forgot to remember my mother's passing.

But I suspect that'd be okay with my mother.

I think of her often and say aloud, "I miss you, Momma," at all sorts of odd times—like when I walk on the beach spearing trash, or when I pull out my Betty Crocker cookbook with the broken binding and turn to page 305 to make a pie crust and see her handwritten recipe for chocolate bittersweets, or when they are wheeling me through the meat-locker-cool corridor that smells like coffee on the way to cataract surgery in the operating room where the Spinners are piped in singing, "Then Came You, Then Came You."

Mostly, I think of her when I slip on her wedding ring, a thin band of gold, before I slide on my own wedding ring of diamonds and gold, which I got out of the habit of wearing when I worked as a massage therapist. But I wear it when I go out, and often wonder, when did my hands become just like my mother's? Although they aren't, really. Hers were stiff with arthritis, which I don't have, but we do share the same kind of thin-skinned, blue-veiny look that telegraphs age.

I slide on her ring whenever I visit doctors, and I am nervous about what they will say, or recommend procedures I probably won't want to do, or when I travel and am afraid that the plane will go down in flames. I want my mother near me—even though she didn't know me for many years before she died, since Alzheimer's gunked up her brain. But I knew her—and I suspect that on some level beyond conscious awareness, she did still know me—at least that's what I like to tell myself.

And I have her energy forever imbued in this skinny band of gold. While I may forget all sorts of important dates in the future, I trust that I'll always remember to slip on my mother's ring to comfort me whenever I need it.

Waiting for Irma

Sunday, September 10, 1:58 p.m.
Rain batters our fragile roof, which has been leaking for the last three months and is now covered with a thin, blue tarp as we wait for repairs. Too late, now. The tarp is in tatters. Rain pounds against the windows. It sounds like bacon frying in a hot skillet—short, staccato beats against the windows.

No newspaper delivery today. That's not a surprise, and yet I *am* surprised by how letdown I feel without our papers. I feel bereft when they are not lying near the back tire of Jim's Toyota in their blue sleeves. Instead, I pull up *The New York Times* on Jim's iPad, which is obviously not a hardship. Nothing like a hurricane looming to bring into sharp relief how wedded I am to my habits: like reading an actual paper newspaper. It just isn't the same on the iPad. Yet, the content is all there—and I go to the Op-Ed section and start a piece, "Trump's War on Science," which is probably a masochistic choice as Hurricane Irma bears down on us.

Yellow and green palm fronds fling themselves against the window on my left. I pause my reading to check on the leaks. The wells in multiple windows are soaking the paper towels I stuffed in them at an alarming rate, and the spare litter box in the fireplace is about one-third full of water. I pull out the litter box carefully to avoid spilling it on the hardwood floor and dump it down the kitchen sink. I set it back in the fireplace—and hear a steady *plop, plop, plop.*

When we first got married, I used to hear Jim clinking ice cubes a floor away, and he liked to say I have the acute hearing of a bat. Now, my ears are twitching, trying to locate the source of those *plop*s. Ah. The closet in the master bedroom. Jim shines the beam from a newly purchased flashlight up to the ceiling, and we stand transfixed, watching drops form, hang for a second, and then plunk to the floor. We unfurl a new tarp of clear vinyl, set four blue bins on top of it, and pad back to our reading stations.

The wind gusts rattle the very bones of the house. I feel uneasy. I consider this deluge a mere squall. We are still hours away from the real show, peak intensity, full onslaught. I wonder: Did we do the right thing to stay here?

We are packed to leave for a pet-friendly shelter, if necessary. By the steps, a mountain grows (one suitcase per adult, a stack of reading material, a waterproof container of our important papers, the cats' rabies certificates, three cat carriers, three cat boxes, dry cat food, litter, Catsby's medication, raingear, sheets, pillows, and sleeping mats), ready to grab and go. But at some point, it won't be safe to leave. The causeways to and from the mainland will close to traffic.

We left during Hurricane Matthew last October to stay in the pet-friendly Homewood Suites in Maitland, just north of Orlando. But this time, despite calling several days ahead, there are no vacancies within a three-hour radius—and we are not leaving our animals. And where would we go? West doesn't work, given the track of the storm. East doesn't work since that's the Atlantic Ocean. North means sitting on the highway with thousands of other evacuees.

Dad calls. I hear the worry in his voice. "We are planning on staying," I say. "We won't be stupid," I say. "We will seek shelter, if necessary." The phone *pings* with texts from friends and family—concerned and caring. The phone *pings* with tornado warnings: *TAKE SHELTER NOW*. A tornado touches down a few miles south of us at Patrick Air Force Base.

Later that night, 7:38 p.m.

As I finish loading the dishwasher with dirty supper dishes, the power goes off. Just like that, it is dark, and the A/C unit shuts off, but the computers beep for several minutes as we scurry around to turn off the auxiliary batteries. Jim says, "It's a lot scarier in the dark." Yes, it is. The winds are intensifying.

Jim is in no hurry to move to the lower-floor room. I am worried, however, about tornadoes touching down around us, about our compromised roof blowing off, about the leaks, and especially about gathering together all three cats in time. The youngest, Catsby, is a master of disappearing. Partly his behavior is just a smart strategy to avoid Cody, who likes to lie in wait for him at the top of the stairs and get in a hiss and a swat or two as Catsby darts by him. Sometimes, though, we can't find Catsby for long stretches of time until he casually shows up for dinner, strolling in from some hidden hidey-hole.

But now, the cats are surprisingly easy to corral. I'm trying to stay calm and not generate that aura of anxiety I do when I'm trying to capture them for a vet visit. Usually, this first-floor room where we are sheltering is off-limits to them, the one place in the house I like to keep fur-free. As my younger brother, Tom, says, "You have cats, you have cat hair." He is right; it is true. Despite our best efforts, it's just part of the deal when you share your home with animal companions.

Now allowed into the forbidden room, the cats are quite happy to explore and sniff new smells, including us, as we grow increasingly pungent with sweat.

Midnight

The storm gathers ferocity—gusts of wind rattle the windows and ill-fitting screens. I lie on top of the sheets, sweaty. I drape a wet dish towel around my neck in a futile attempt to cool down. Cody comes by for a pat now and then, and I hug him close until he purrs. Then I release him. Jim snores. I yell at one point, "Stop it!" He snorts, turns over, and starts to snore again. In my head, I keep trying to find words to describe the sound of the wind. It's kind of like a nor'easter, but not quite. It's got a howling quality to it that is unique, unlike anything I've ever heard before. The house trembles. I wake Jim, and we go upstairs, flashlights illuminating the way, to check on the leaks. Rain is gushing in through the balcony doors in the master bedroom. On hands and knees, I sop up water and wring out towels while Jim duct-tapes dry towels in place. It feels futile. We empty the container from the fireplace again, refresh paper towels in the window wells, and go back downstairs to pass the night.

Jim snores. The cats walk on my head and pull my hair. I am scared but not terrified. It's also kind of exciting. It's all so elemental. I feel an urge to dash outside and get whipped around in the wind, but good sense prevails, and I stay put. The wind moans in frequencies I've never heard before. I must have fallen asleep, because then it's daybreak.

Monday, September 11, 7 a.m.

It is quiet. That's the first thing I notice. Jim is gone, but not sucked up and out through a hole in the roof—just outside, clearing debris. All three cats lie around me on the bed, like points of a triangle, not in the least perturbed. Six eyes stare at me.

I open the front door and go out to the voices. Our neighbor says, "Ray lost his roof." We wander up the street. It is true. Ray's roof is in the tree next door to his decapitated house. We offer our condolences and our support. It feels so puny. Along A1A, street signs bow to the ground, and telephone wires lie in the road. Cops block through traffic. Trees recline on their sides, roots hanging in the air. Swales overflow with water. A fine layer of sand and salt covers everything. The landscape, usually lush and green, is now gray and brown.

Tuesday, September 12, 10:15 p.m.

The lights come back on, and the fans, and the A/C unit rumbles back to life. Our neighbor texts, "Thank you, to the heavens above." We sleep in the cool air and delight in having to pull up a sheet to cover our shoulders, feeling a tad chilly.

Wednesday, September 13, 11:30 a.m.

Oh, no! The power goes off again. The good news is that the water comes on a few hours later, just minutes after Jim returns from the public park down the road in Satellite Beach with four, five-gallon containers full of water, twenty gallons in total, enough for multiple toilet flushes. I have been constipated for days, worried about adding my refuse to the already compromised sewer system.

Thursday, September 14, 3:46 p.m.

The newspaper says Florida Power & Light Company (FPL) hopes to restore power by the end of the weekend. We are resigning ourselves to another couple of hot, humid, sweat-filled days and nights. However, when I come home from a yoga class (with A/C and where a woman I know only casually offers her spare bedroom for as long as we need it), Jim is dancing in the driveway. Could it be? Yes, it is. The power is back on. Thank you to the heavens above!

After Irma

After Irma, I've noticed a couple of things. Recovery is slow, slow, slow. It takes a lot longer than we want or expect, another tangible reminder that our infrastructure is inadequate (as is skilled labor). But as it turns out, the physical stuff is the easier part to deal with. We get a new roof. In several closets, the stinky, moldy drywall, an alarming black, is torn out, and they are completely renovated in mid-February, about five months after Irma hit. We consider ourselves fortunate. Many of our neighbors still await repairs. They are stuck with blue tarps doing a half-assed job covering their leaks during our frequent, drenching downpours, and some of them still can't live in their homes.

The emotional damage lingers like that achy tooth I just can't stop worrying with my tongue. For weeks after Irma, it is like my neighbors aren't fully here. They aren't as transparent as apparitions, but it is as though a piece of them that tethered them to the earth slipped away and isn't fully back yet—at least that's how it feels. And whenever it rains, an anxiousness steals over me as I wander around the house mewling softly to myself, checking and double-checking all the places where it previously leaked, conditioned to expect the worst. I hope that over time I will once again come to enjoy the sound of rain.

After Irma, I find myself wondering, too, about what is vital, what is so important to me, so precious I couldn't live without it. Think about it. If you had to evacuate, what would you take—realizing all might be lost, and you might not have a home to return to, everything swept away or damaged beyond repair? For me, it boiled down to the husband, the cats, one box of vital papers (passports, Jim's divorce decree, our marriage certificate, birth certificates), albums of family photos, a collection of love letters Jim's parents wrote to each other during their courtship and World War II, and a few pieces of jewelry, including my mother's wedding ring.

Perhaps, what most endures from living through Irma is just that—the experience of living through it. We now have a felt sense of the horrible anticipation that arises when a ferocious storm bears down, as well as that moment of awakening in the aftermath, when a brilliant sun shines, but everything is forever altered. Now we know what it feels like to live with uncertainty and be in the dark, where our imaginations run wild and rarely spin out best-case scenarios. Now we know what it feels like to live without electricity and water and internet connections and have no clue as to when they will be restored. Now we know what it feels like to have no idea when normalcy will once again be the norm. What will be the long-term effects? I haven't a clue, but I like to tell myself that we now have an increased capacity for compassion and empathy for anyone displaced from their home—which can only be a good thing.

This World Will Break
Your Heart

A merican Airlines flight 1593 touches down on the short runway of National Airport and comes to an abrupt stop. I snap the Washington Monument from the window while we wait to deplane. It's a lousy photo, but it does its job—it anchors me in familiar territory.

The primary purpose of this trip is not to tramp the familiar streets of D.C., nor see old friends, nor explore the many delights of the city, but to visit my Aunt Celie, long my favorite aunt. She was recently diagnosed with aggressive lung cancer and given a really shitty prognosis.

I brave the madness of Metro D.C. traffic and navigate the rental car up the George Washington Parkway to 495 and then to 270 to 40 to 15 to the Rosemont Avenue exit in Frederick. After a few miles and some deep breaths, I relax enough to ease the death grip on the steering wheel to fiddle with the side mirrors and the radio. Finding nothing to my liking, I turn it off, which leaves me alone with my thoughts—dangerous territory to wander alone. However, the heavy traffic whizzing by on the left and the right means my focus needs to stay razor-sharp.

I pull up to the curb outside my aunt's house. I am going for a smooth glide in, but misjudge the distance and hit the curb with a jolt. No damage done, however, and my aunt greets me at the kitchen door. Right after I step over the threshold into that familiar kitchen where I spent umpteen number of hours sitting at the table yakking with Aunt Celie and my grandmother during my four years of college down the street, she offers me vegetable soup, homemade, of course. I decline, but the offer has done its job—brought me smack-dab into the present moment with my aunt. There is no place I would rather be than in her excellent company. But it's not just about nostalgia, although her influence on me was *huge* (and healing), her steady feminine presence offsetting my troubled relationship with my mother. No, it was always more than that. She was, then, and still is a formidable force in her own right—and today, she wears a T-shirt that reads, *Never underestimate an OLD WOMAN who graduated from FHS, Frederick High School.* Never underestimate this woman, indeed.

I haven't seen my aunt since my mother's memorial celebration in June of 2011, but the intervening years dissolve in an instant. I feel welcomed, loved, and accepted in Aunt Celie's presence. During this visit, I discover others feel the same way. In a text with her daughter, my cousin Betsy, when I comment on the kindness of Aunt Celie's housecleaner, who showed up with chicken pot pies for dinner as I was leaving, Betsy replied, "Mom always brings out the best in people." I hope somebody says that about me someday.

However lovely the visit, which it is, I am acutely aware that Aunt Celie is mortal—as am I.

This mortality thing has been smacking me in the face lately. At my doctor's insistence, I recently got a mammogram. Then a week later, I got the dreaded letter in the mail saying there were some *abnormalities* and additional procedures were recommended.

Four visits later to my doctor's office, I finally have the necessary orders with the correct procedural codes. And after ponying up $439.23 for the deductible over the phone (despite being told by our insurance company it would only be $200), and after hurling a fit of pique at the registration lady, "We need to do something in this country to fix our broken healthcare system. Each year we pay more and more for lousier coverage. Please vote Democratic," and then after apologizing for misdirecting my anger towards her, she calls the hospital specially to see if she can get me in earlier than her screen says is available. Then voilà, I am scheduled for my additional procedures. Touched by her kindness, I gush thanks.

But they are inconclusive, and now the radiologist wants to do a biopsy. What he says makes sense, and he tells me not to be unduly alarmed—but still, I wonder if this is overkill. Then when I find out it's going to cost us $871 (the rest of the deductible and co-pay) towards the $4,000 total cost (yes, $4,000 for a stereotactic biopsy), I *really* wonder if it's overkill. Fibrocystic breast disease runs in the family, and I do not expect anything to be seriously wrong. Still, it's hard not to be alarmed, and I have to coax my shoulders to drop down from up around my ears.

My heart breaks so easily these days, like the fragile bird eggs that fall out of nests and lie cracked on the ground in spring. I suspect it's a natural function of aging and living a full-out life. But my heart mends easily, too. Little acts of consideration and kindness go a long way. There is such goodness in the world, and I see it clearly when I tune to that frequency. It feels imperative these days to focus on the good to help bind up the cracked and broken places.

Back in D.C., the next day, on my way to the Outliers and American Vanguard Art exhibit at the National Gallery of Art, I glance at my phone and see my aunt has called. I duck into the deserted concrete plaza of the Canadian Embassy to muffle the sounds of busy Pennsylvania Avenue and call her back.

More sad news. My cousin David has succumbed to the flu, alone in his house in Waynesboro, Pennsylvania. Betsy and her husband, Scott, drove to his home, increasingly alarmed after not being able to reach him by phone. They arrived to see a bag of groceries on his porch, left by a neighbor, and immediately suspected the worst. They called the police. When the police arrived, Betsy waited in the car, and Scott entered the house with the cops, where they saw—and smelled—David dead in the bathroom. A jolt shoots through my body when my aunt tells me this. I feel bad for Scott and Betsy and, of course, for David. I feel deep sorrow, too, even though I haven't seen David in years.

He was always tall and thin, but the last time I saw him, he was skinny as a stick and bearded like a mountain man living in isolation. My aunt would share news about David from time to time. I knew he was an excellent and avid golfer and often played with Scott, but we weren't close. At family gatherings, David blended into the background, quiet and reserved, more observer than participant, as his gaggle of girl cousins chattered and laughed around him. Now faced with his untimely demise, I wish I'd made more of an effort to get to know him better—to love him better. Still, he mattered to us. He was part of us. I hope he knew that.

Family, including my younger brother, Tom, and friends, will lay David to eternal rest on what would have been his sixtieth birthday. From afar, I mourn David Winfield VanFossen's too-early death. Death, like spilled ink, spreads into my generation.

Later that evening, my last in D.C., I swing by the National Portrait Gallery and take my place in the queue to see the Obama portraits. There is a palpable excitement in the crowd of people waiting to snap selfies with Michelle and Barack. I send Jim a text: *I miss the Obamas.*

Then, on my way to the hotel, I glide up the escalator from the bowels of the Foggy Bottom Metro Station into the chilly evening and see a young, dark-haired woman—a girl really—in a heavy coat, sitting cross-legged on the sidewalk with two large dogs, one tan, one a mottled gray, curled around her. She holds a sign with a too-common message, *Homeless, Hungry, Need Money.* I bend down to give her a dollar, and my heart hurts as she says, "Thanks," and I take in the scene, the blanket, how calm the dogs are, like this is just another typical evening.

This world will break your heart if you let it. But what choice do we have? Sorrow, anxiety, anger, powerlessness—it's all part of the deal. And while I wouldn't necessarily seek any of those emotions deliberately, they do sharpen my appreciation for the little kindnesses and the beauty that is all around.

I am back in Florida now. Our local meteorologist, Mallory Nicholls, reports we are unseasonably cold. Still, it's in the mid-sixties, hardly cold-cold by most measures. Out the porch door, against a brilliant, azure sky, palm fronds bob and weave in a brisk breeze, ducks glide across the pond, and an anhinga stands on the bank, its wings spread wide to dry. Behind me, Cayce and Catsby roll and tussle and then settle down in the rays that the sun throws across the bed. Cody naps atop Jim's dirty underwear and opens one eye and rumbles with a soft purr when I lay my head on him. For just a moment or two, I let my vibrations sync up with his before I continue with my day.

Laundry

I climb the steps from the garage to the living room: one, two, three, four, five, six, seven ... all the way to twenty. The cat barrels through the 4-Way-Locking Cat Flap, which no longer locks any which way, and dashes by me on the right, clearly not counting the number of steps he barely touches with his fleet-feet.

Carrying a bin overflowing with clean clothes just out of the dryer, I walk over to the dining room table, shove the newspapers cluttering the table to one side, and set the laundry down with a *thunk* in the center of my husband's place mat, streaked dark with inky newsprint. Then I get to work folding the warm clothes: T-shirts and sheets and pillowcases, which never quite lose the scent of my husband. I bury my face in one of those cases and inhale deeply; his smell calms me.

I sort my undies from my husband's, although he'd never call his underpants *undies*. On more than one occasion, he pulls a pastel pair of my silky panties from his underwear bin stuck to a pair of his white cotton jockeys.

I ask, "Would you like to wear them on your head?" He demurs and tosses them to me to catch, which I do, although no one would ever describe me as athletically inclined. I am particularly bad at catching. Toss a ball to me, or a lemon, or a set of keys, and my hands turn into rigid ice sculptures with fingers I expect to snap off when struck.

Back in junior high, during one misbegotten spring, I tried out for the softball team. I stood way out in left field, praying the ball would come nowhere near me. It didn't, and the coach eliminated me in the first cut—expected, but still a disappointment.

I was an uncoordinated teen, despite years of dance lessons at Verlene's and then Angela's Dance Studio in Broadalbin, New York, the tiny upstate town of my youth. It's a wonder, isn't it, that this town of 2,500 inhabitants could support one, let alone two, dance studios? But back then, there were passels of little wannabee ballerinas dreaming of gracefully twirling in stiff tutus on a stage before an adoring audience rising to their feet and shouting, "Bravo! Bravo!" as the finale drew to a close.

During junior high, I danced, at least after a fashion, at the Catholic rec center in town on Friday nights, and recall a sweaty palm or two pressed up against mine as strobe lights flashed around us to the driving sound of the Bee Gees. How could anyone resist moving to the disco beat? But sneaking cigs and swigging cheap wine held much more appeal than any moves I might cut on the dance floor.

There is visual proof in an old photo album that I danced on the cusp of early adulthood with my father at a dad and daughter weekend during college. I don't recall any huge gaffes, so I think it's safe to assume we did okay and didn't embarrass ourselves. I suspect that was partly due to a band that played songs allowing us to stick to the dance steps we knew, me from junior high ballroom dance classes, and my father from army USO dances. No wild winging it at Hood College with Dad was required.

But a couple of decades later, a friend made fun of me at a company affair when I danced. That did it for me— the end of dancing. I wonder now if my kneejerk reaction wasn't misplaced. Perhaps what I was stung by was a supposed good friend mocking me, and my so-called dancing was merely the catalyst for a moment of casual cruelty. Nonetheless, in that moment, I decided Beth and dancing could no longer be partners.

Since that unfortunate night, I lock up as soon as the first strains of music waft through the air, fearful I will be Elaine on *Seinfeld*, all rigid limbs akimbo, co-workers and strangers snickering behind my back. It is a miserable hangover I can't shake, and it makes me dread that part of wedding receptions and class reunions when the band strikes up the music, and I'll be expected—or asked—to dance.

I suppose I could just say the truth, "No thanks, I don't want to dance," and be done with it. Why is that so hard? Maybe because it's not really true. My body *likes* to move. I tap my toes and snap my fingers to any jazzy beat, but then that darn self-consciousness rears up, and the fear of looking stupid wins out—like anyone is really looking at me. But you never know, do you? Maybe they are.

I wonder how often we stifle our creative impulses out of fear of what others will think. All that potential unrealized. It's kind of sad, isn't it? All that energy squashed because of the fear of looking ridiculous and wearing the proverbial scarlet "S" of shame.

For instance, right now, with folded piles of laundry growing on the table, I could parade around the living room to a John Sousa march cranked up high, with underwear on my head, and no one would be the wiser—except for our three cats, who could shield their eyes with their paws if they found the spectacle too upsetting.

Instead, I stick to the routine and do not sway to any beat. I wash clothes, dry clothes, and match up sweet-smelling socks still toasty from the dryer, all the while thinking of an old boyfriend, Gray. Recently, I surprised him with a call on his birthday, catching him at work when I expected just to leave a message. I sputtered all over myself when he answered, but we soon fell into the natural rhythm of old friends as we caught up on the fifteen years that have passed since we've seen each other.

He was gregarious Gray with the naturally curly, reddish-brown hair that caught streaks of the sun during the summers we spent together in Rehoboth Beach, Delaware. I loved his springy hair shot through with gold. It is gray, now, he said.

He was a blind date that turned out great for several years until one Christmas, when I was expecting an engagement ring—and instead, he gave me a copper pot. It was an expensive, high-end copper pot, but still—it was a copper pot. It was evident in that moment he didn't want to marry me, then or ever. He did, however, subsequently marry another really nice woman, and I another really nice man.

But way before marriages—and kids (for him), and cats (for me), and dogs (for him)—on one of our early dates, Gray came to pick me up wearing a red L.L. Bean flannel shirt, which was soft to the touch and made me want to stroke him like a cat all night. When we turned to leave the house, I noticed something stuck to one sleeve—a dark sock, probably recently out of his dryer. I plucked it off and handed it to him.

He laughed and said, "I am a wild and crazy guy." And then Gray made a couple of funny dance moves, all alternating arms and fingers and hip switches from side to side, just like Steve Martin did with his partner, Dan Aykroyd, on *SNL* a bazillion years ago.

A wild and crazy guy. What if I could be a wild and crazy gal? What would that even look like? I know one thing I'd like—a devil-may-care attitude—especially when it comes to my body, especially when it comes to my *aging* body.

However, I doubt I'm going to change my basic stripes any time soon. Still, I would like to dance, or feel like I *can* dance without looking like I am committing a crime against nature at those inevitable events that beg for a communal experience.

Surely this is not an insurmountable obstacle. What to do? What to do?

What about refresher dance lessons? That's an idea. I like structure. I like being a student. I have a partner. I am teachable. At least I was in junior high. Perhaps lessons could provide a helpful framework where I could re-learn specific steps, and then possibly progress to the freedom to improvise. Something to consider. What's the worst that could happen?

Rarely, if ever, do I regret trying something new. Nope, just the opposite; it's the missed chances, the opportunities I didn't grab hold of, or pursue that spark pangs of regret. And there is always that possibility I would enjoy myself.

As I finish folding the laundry, I think back again to Gray, and the sock stuck to his red shirt and his jokey reaction. He was such a good-natured guy, and I bet he still is. Immediately following his brief performance as a wild and crazy guy on that long-ago evening, he laughed, then I laughed, and then we laughed together, as we opened up the door and stepped out into the night where everything was possible.

The Day Before Valentine's Day

It is nearly noon on February 13, the day before Valentine's Day, and I still wear my pajamas, a fleece twinset with a royal-blue background, splashed with a symmetrical pattern of large white snowflakes. I love these jammies, which I only get to wear a couple of days every year, since it's generally way too warm for fleece in Florida. But during that occasional cold snap when I do wear them, I marvel at the snowflake symmetry woven into the fabric, the repeating pattern of exactitude, which never happens in nature.

Rare too would be the sight of snowflakes falling on palm trees in Florida—although it happened once on this slender barrier island off the east coast of Central Florida, my man and I have called home for more than thirteen years. That day, I was on the phone with my father. It was his first conversation of the morning, his first spoken words to another human being, so he repeatedly and with gusto cleared his throat to loosen up the phlegm and activate his vocal cords, hacking loudly and directly into the receiver, like he always does. And, like I always do, I moved the phone away from my ear and said, "Dad, that's loud! You're hurting my ears!" But it never makes any difference. During subsequent morning phone calls, he does the same thing; he seems incapable of moving the receiver a few inches. Oh, well!

My father, like all of us, is full of contradictions. He was a Phi Beta Kappa college valedictorian in physics but has never once pumped his own gas, or used an ATM, and he was generally hapless around the house. Lawns he could mow, and did, including our wide, expansive front, side, and back yards (always with a push mower sweating profusely, pulling out his ubiquitous, all-pur-pose handkerchief to sop up that sweat). And for several winters when I was a kid, he flooded a side yard during our frigid, upstate New York winters to provide a small skating rink for my brothers, himself, and me to twirl around on. But competently completing general house repairs? Forget about it. The fix-it stuff, like repairing a running toilet, that was a job for the pros.

So, on that morning, I tamped down my annoyance at his amplified throat clearing. It's a tiny irritation offset by the privilege of hanging out with the "old guy," as he calls himself.

While specific details about that conversation are lost to the ethers, we likely talked about what we usually talk about: books (probably about his latest Science of Mind book-group selection), movies, politics, and the sorry state of the country, when right in the middle of a sentence—after what I imagine to be an in-sync, rueful shake of our heads as, 1,287 miles apart, we were united in feeling powerless to change some very big things that needed changing—we dangled our conversation when I said, "It's snowing." And then, for no longer than ninety seconds or so, flurries fell on palm trees and sand dunes, and the feathers of the sandpipers scurrying up the beach. It was bizarre that snow falling on our beachy shores, and for a few minutes, everything was surreal, with my attention heightened like a freshly sharpened cleaver.

Dad likes to talk about the weather. When we discuss it, I hear a crispness in his tone, and not only because it's a safe, neutral topic, although I suspect that's part of the appeal. On more than one occasion growing up, after a charged outburst from my mother or me, he called feelings "those damn emotions," looking like he'd prefer to be anywhere but near the two of us.

The appeal of weather for him is old and harkens to his WWII years, when, in February 1943, he enlisted in the army, shortly after turning eighteen, to study meteorology. He wanted to be a weatherman, but that wasn't meant to be. After he spent a year in the army's program, they concluded they had overestimated the number of meteorologists needed and transferred Dad into training in radar and electronics—which also turned out to be an excellent fit. First, the army sent him to Ontario, Canada, to study, and then to a select program at the Massachusetts Institute of Technology in Cambridge, where he was housed in a dorm rather than barracks (and very thankful for that). Then, he was sent to teach as a radar instructor at various locations throughout the States, including Fort Dix in New Jersey and Shaw Air Force Base in Sumter, South Carolina.

I always thought my father hated the army, and when I called him recently to verify the facts, one of the first things he said was how long he'd served, "Two years, ten months, and sixteen days." But he didn't say it like it was a jail sentence, more just reciting the facts, and he went on to say that being in the army was a good experience.

"What did you like about it?" I asked.

"I learned a lot about math, physics, and liberal arts. I earned credits that transferred to college when I went, which was paid for by the G.I. Bill. I was grateful not to be sent overseas to fight," he said. "I was happy to do my part." And, with that last sentence, that's when I feel a moment of clarity slice through our conversation—the truth of a higher calling—his small part to help save the world from the Nazis.

So, while "Willie with the Weather" wasn't meant to be his career, it has been an avocation, punctuated with a heightened interest in fierce storms since his only daughter moved to hurricane country.

While hurricanes are definitely a concern, hurricane season officially ended on November 30. Winter in Florida is a reprieve, even though this one is unseasonably wet and cold. The damp conditions invite sloth, and I lounge around in pajamas and my gray fleece robe, a comfortable but unflattering puffy thing from J. Jill that makes me look like a genderless blob belted in the middle. I think Jim still finds me attractive. However, it's hard to know because he's never been big on giving compliments. But we have an easy physicality between us (people on the street have stopped us on more than one occasion to tell us how cute we are holding hands, which, while well-intentioned, makes me feel about a hundred years old), and I suspect I would know if he found me repulsive.

Just a few hours ago, on this chilly Saturday morning, which is still way above freezing, and without any hint of snow flurries this day before Valentine's Day, Jim lifts his bicycle overhead and sets it on the tracks on top of his car, snaps the security bars into place, and backs out of the driveway, scraping low-hanging branches that shower down brown, gold, and green leaves. I watch him from the bedroom window, with Cody-cat slung over my shoulder, and before Jim makes a right turn at the end of the driveway and fades from view, I call out, "Be careful out there."

Knowing Jim will be gone for several hours, Cody and I pad up to the third-floor office to pay bills and write. He joins his two brothers to loll in a ray of sunshine slanting diagonally across the bedspread as I clack away on the computer, going silent at regular intervals, distracted by the news of the day. Then I hear a click as a key turns the lock in the front door, and the rubber strip on the bottom of the door drags across the tile floor as the door is shoved open. My heart skips a beat or two. *Who the hell is that?* I lean over the railing and see a man coming up the steps. My pulse returns to normal when I spot the familiar bald head on top of Jim's hefty frame.

He carries a riot of color in his hands—yellow and white and red and purple flowers and pink lilies that dominate the bouquet with their size and sweet aroma. Pink is my favorite color. Jim is a man who may be short on giving out compliments, but one who nevertheless pays attention, at least sometimes, to the whims, likes, and dislikes of his wife.

Three cats and I pad down the steps. I say, "They are beautiful." I am dee-lighted and consider bursting into song—maybe "Oh, what a beautiful mornin', Oh, what a beautiful day," but the moment passes, since my singing skills are more scratchy-warble than sweeping aria, and instead, I smooch Jim on the lips. He sets the flowers down on the coffee table in the living room.

Shortly thereafter, he leaves again, this time to pedal his bike along the river for real. His Valentine's Day duty is done for another year. I imagine he lets out a little sigh of relief.

The house falls quiet again. The cats wait patiently, like cats do, just an occasional twitch of the tail to break their statue-like stillness, biding their time until I ascend again to the top floor and resume tapping the keyboard. I eventually comply, and then in nearly but not quite perfect unison (which I watch surreptitiously over the railing), they jump up on the table to sniff the bouquet of flowers.

A Death in the Family

My brothers, Tom and Bill, eye their assigned seats in the front row, and then squish in next to the other pallbearers. Jim and I slide in behind them in the second row. The guys' broad shoulders strain against their suit jackets, and I wonder if the seams will hold. We are early, and every couple of minutes, I swivel my head around to see what's going on. We stand to hug relatives we haven't seen in years. One cousin, still tall and skinny, sports a full gray beard. It's a good look on him. The chapel fills slowly, and then nearly to capacity by 11 a.m., the start time.

My Aunt Celie, my mother's youngest sister, the matriarch at the center of our family, is gone.

That phrase, *matriarch at the center of our family*, sprang unbidden from my fingers clacking away on the keyboard. Why? What does that even mean? I think it boils down to two main attributes: providing an emotional center and wielding power.

"Empathetic. One smart cookie." That's how my father described Aunt Celie when I asked for his opinion.

And I think he'd add *attractive* (she was the sole brunette in a sea of redheads, and my father is a fan of dark-haired beauties, at least those on the big screen), *athletic* (first as a basketball player and then as a referee), and *confident*.

Her home was a tangible example of an emotional center. It was open to most of her large, extended family and always smelled of something good to eat—homemade vegetable soup simmering on the stove, a sheet of chocolate chip cookies or a peach pie just out of the oven, cooling on a metal rack. And her caring crossed generations. I visited one day and found her brother, an old man, his health slipping further and further away, sitting at her kitchen table nursing a second cup of coffee. Uncle Bub was just hanging out with his sister, not looking for anything specific, but knowing he'd feel better by being there—as I did. Steps away, past the pantry and the powder room, in a corner of the dining room, a group of wee ones played with the stash of toys she kept specifically for their pleasure.

My aunt, however, was also human and thus carried at least *one* contradiction. She'd tossed a long-term relationship with a sister-in-law into the trash bin when she concluded her brother had been wronged. There was no reasoning with her about this (at least by me), any nuances lost to stark black-and-white thinking: brother good, sister-in-law bad. It didn't rise (or fall?) to Hatfield-McCoy-level animosity, but, still, I found it disquieting. I could never reconcile her willingness to amputate some family members from her life with the big-hearted, generous aunt-love I knew. And, I always had a teensy bit of fear that someday I might do something inadvertently that would result in my banishment from my aunt's good graces. Once out, you were not welcome back in.

Yet, who isn't flawed? I have some serious character deficits, and people still love me. And I loved my aunt, despite (and maybe because of?) her not being perfect.

She had great presence and warmth—or at least that's what she projected to this niece, and she did wield power, in accordance with the other part of my informal definition of *matriarch*. On numerous occasions, my aunt stood up to my mother, who was nineteen years older than her sister and a formidable woman in her own right. My mother criticized her sister's bad habits (like smoking), as well as matters of her heart. As a teenager, my aunt was dead set on marrying a man my mother disapproved of, hurling this at her, "You'd never marry Harry if Daddy were alive!" Guess what my aunt did? Yup, she married Harry. Even if my mother was right (certainly she was about my aunt's smoking), I admired my aunt's moxie in taking her on.

During one particularly ugly screaming match between my mother and me (probably over my misbehaving boyfriend, Vince), Aunt Celie sat with me at the kitchen table. We just sat together, as she calmly smoked her Winstons, until my hands stopped trembling, and I quit muttering, "I hate her."

Where did that self-possession come from? It may have something to do with the loss of her father when

Celie was just nine years old. My grandfather's death at forty-nine was certainly a shock to my mother. She was twenty-eight, married, pregnant, and living about an hour away in a suburb of Baltimore with my father, a young engineer at Bendix, and their first child, my older brother Bill, then a toddler. My mother miscarried shortly after receiving the news, and while her father's death may not be *the* factor, it was certainly *a* factor when she lost that baby.

So, circumstances out of my nine-year-old aunt's control forced her to grow up fast. She had to support her mother, not just emotionally but also with day-to-day tasks. Family lore goes that, before my grandfather died, my grandmother had never even written a check, which I suspect was more a reflection of the times than of her abilities. My grandmother was quite resilient and took boarders into the large, commodious colonial my grandfather built on a picturesque street in Frederick, Maryland, a block away from Culler Lake, to help support her and her young daughter.

I loved visiting my grandmother and aunt, and especially going to that lake as a kid. That meant, one, hanging out with Aunt Celie, and, two, feeding the ducks. A double treat! Like an ice cream cone with a decadent second scoop! As soon as Aunt Celie and I crossed the road and started down the slightly sloping walk to the water's edge, bags of stale bread swinging by our sides, quacking ducks waddled up to us, nipping our fingertips, anticipating the bread crumbs we were about to toss their way.

My aunt was always central in my life. After a brief early marriage to Harry—a tall, dark, and handsome guy, whose good looks I remember well—she married for a second time to Charlie (also a good-looking man but blonde), and had, by all accounts, a long, happy union. I remember when she was pregnant with the first of their two children. I was sixteen and heard my mother talking on the phone with her sister shortly after she gave birth to Betsy; my aunt was ravenous, chowing down on a hamburger.

Aunt Celie and Uncle Charlie lived with my grandmother in the house my grandfather built, and it was the hub for all our family visits. Our own little Lambdin offshoot did not vacation to the ocean, or anywhere, really. When my father took occasional time off from his busy jobs, he drove his family eight hours from our home in upstate New York to Maryland, where we stayed with and visited relatives from the home base of 205 Lindbergh Avenue.

Always, I coveted a place at that kitchen table, the heart of the household, where the adults sat, smoked, drank, laughed—and always seemed to know something I didn't. As a teen, I cautiously slid into a seat at the table, catching my aunt's eye. She would give me a silent nod and a smile of assent, telling me that, *Yes*, I was welcome there.

I'd slide my butt into that seat for years afterwards on a regular basis after I decided to go to college a couple of blocks down the street. My college chums and I were *always* welcome at Lindbergh Avenue, even though my aunt now had a new baby (Jimmy) to care for. Now it was my turn to take a youngster (Betsy, a toddler) to the park and feed the ducks. I also took Betsy over to the college to show her off, where she was determined to climb the steep flights of steps on her own up to my dorm room. But, mostly, my friends and I swarmed their house. Did I ever call in advance? I don't think so, and yet we were always warmly greeted. My aunt was never too busy or too distracted to set aside whatever she was doing to spend time with my friends and me. One night, she sobbed with us through *Love Story*, as we arrayed ourselves around the TV set on the living room's thick, pile carpet like bouquets of spring flowers. What a gift to my friends and me!

Wasn't I fortunate to have such an influential aunt in my life? My father recently suggested she was a mother-in-residence for me while I was at college. That's probably true, but the relationship may have been even a bit more complicated. Perhaps she was an amalgam of a mother that I didn't always find wanting, like my own, and the older sister I never had but always wanted. Aunt Celie was, after all, only eleven years older than I.

After college, I never visited in the same casual way. Still, when I did visit, or when we spoke, the intervening years evaporated like fog in the sunshine, and we tumbled into an easy rapport. I've since learned that kind of relationship is not common and is something to treasure.

Now, a little over four decades later, on a blustery Saturday in mid-October, the sun peeking in and out of clouds darting across the sky, we are saying goodbye to

Aunt Celie. In the short ceremony, the pastor reads a couple of poems. A few of us speak, and, as a group, we recite the Lord's Prayer. Then the funeral home attendants slide into position to usher us quietly out of this sacred space, row by row, starting with the pallbearers. The seams of the guys' suit jackets have held.

We file silently out of the funeral home and then burst into awkward conversations on the porch as we wait to take our assigned places in the procession of cars to Mt. Olivet Cemetery, a short ride away. During the brief graveside service, we shiver in the cold air while fierce winds blow up the ladies' too-thin fancy dresses— and then it's over. It really is goodbye. I wait in line to tap my aunt's casket a final time.

Then Tom folds his six-foot-three frame into the front seat of Bill's car, Jim and I stuff ourselves into the backseat, and we prepare for the long drive to Saratoga Springs, New York, to see our elderly father, too frail to make the trip for his sister-in-law's funeral. We three sibs have not spent unbroken hours together like this in years (if ever). During the conversation-soaked trip, which keeps circling back to stories and memories of Aunt Celie, I consider how much I not only love my brothers but how much I genuinely *like* them. We drop Tom off at his SUV in a parking lot not far from Binghamton, and when he steps out of the car, I say, "I'm sorry we had to be together under such sad circumstances, but I am so glad to have shared this time with you." And then Tom, my athletic, hammer-throwing, "little" brother, pulls me into his arms in one of his great, enveloping Tom-hugs. Now a trio, Bill, Jim, and I continue on for another three hours through a gorgeous part of New York on a spectacular fall day, the setting sun spotlighting the fiery colors of fall dotting the foothills of the Adirondacks we pass by. Does my spiky, acute grief heighten my appreciation for the beauty all around me? Maybe.

A few days later, back in Florida, I post a picture on Facebook. It's of Dad and me, which I took in his apartment. When I post it, my first thought is, *Aunt Celie is going to love this picture.* And then reality hits like a dash of cold water to my face, and I realize, *Nope, that isn't going to happen.* It feels crappy—that moment of realization that my aunt is no longer here. She was the first person I called from the nursing home moments after my mother took her raspy, last breath on a bitterly cold day in late February of 2011. Losing a parent, no matter how complicated the relationship (and ours was), is challenging, and it helped tremendously to have my aunt on the other end of the phone expressing concern and sorrow. She knew our history and loved us both.

Since October of 2017, after the death of Aunt Dolores (the middle sister), Aunt Celie formally assumed the mantle of the matriarch, but honestly, she'd been in that role for years. She was the glue that held us all together, the magnet that attracted us to the house on Lindbergh Avenue. Until the end, we coveted her presence. In one of her last conversations, she said she was feeling well enough to see her fifteen-year-old granddaughter, Riley, play tennis. I bet that tennis match felt more complete to Riley (and Riley's mother, Betsy) because my aunt was there. That was certainly true for me at my mother's memorial service.

The stories I heard shared at Aunt Celie's viewing and funeral confirmed that my experiences with my aunt were more the norm than the exception. There was a common theme among a gaggle of nieces and nephews and great-nieces and great-nephews (and her son-in-law) that they, too, felt they had a "special" relationship with Aunt Celie. From those stories, I learned that none of us were special—because all of us were special.

My aunt's death has been supremely disorienting. I still know up-and-down and right-from-left, but there's an internal something that's just off—my heart has been severely dinged, if not torn asunder. It aches—physically aches. It's hard for me to fully accept she isn't here and won't be here to call on when future loss strikes—like when my father dies. And while I don't expect he'll shuffle off this mortal coil tomorrow, he is nearly ninety-four. Tick-tock, tick-tock.

A part of me watches myself going through the early stages of grief, especially shock and anger, and I know they are not linear; I'll cycle back into them at random times as I move into the next stage. It's easier at times to be mad rather than sad, and I am unduly sharp over stupid stuff—like snapping at Jim when he asks me three times when *Dr. Who* is on—a show I don't even watch. Then, if past experience is any guide, one day, with no warning, this barbed-wire grief will soften into something more tolerable, a duller ache.

The day before Aunt Celie died, I picked up a book I'd had on reserve at the Cocoa Beach Library. It was *American Wolf: A True Story of Survival and Obsession in the West*, by Nate Blakeslee, the *PBS NewsHour* book selection for October. I didn't take that book on the trip to Maryland for my aunt's funeral. Instead, I packed Bill Bryson's *In a Sunburned Country*, his travelogue about his misadventures in Australia, knowing on some level that what I would need in the hotel room over those nights was not a heavy lift, but something lighter, maybe even comic. Bryson did not disappoint, and one night I'm quite sure I dribbled pee while reading a funny passage to Jim. While he found the segment amusing, I found it hilarious—my laughter bordering on hysteria—and he looked at me, a tad concerned, like I was losing it. Maybe I was.

When we got back home, I picked up *American Wolf* and got sucked into the compelling tale of just what's been going on with the wolves since they were reintroduced to Yellowstone in 1995. The author focuses on a few wolves, in particular, to tell a story of competing interests among hunters, the wolves, the feds, local and state governments, various agencies, and the public, including dedicated wolf-watchers.

As I read on, I felt more and more dread, which resulted in less and less sleep and more and more dog-eared pages to share with Jim the next evening after work. I knew it would be hard to read those pages out loud that got to me the most, but still, I felt driven to do it.

When reading to him, I am wracked by grief and have to stop several times to compose myself and let the sobs subside before continuing on about an alpha female who is shot and killed, legally, by a hunter coveting another trophy. I have to read that line twice, the trophy part. But this is no random wolf, which would still be sad, especially to the devoted wolf-watchers and readers like me. This wolf is O-Six (832AF to researchers), a beloved favorite of the Yellowstone community. O-Six has been a central character throughout the stories in the book, and we have come to know her as empathetic, wise, merciful, smart, and resourceful—the matriarch of her pack. When O-Six is killed, her partner remains by her side, silent at first, and then he throws his head back and howls. Soon other members of the Lamar Canyon Pack emerge from the woods to join him, their mournful voices raised together and echoing throughout the wintry, Wyoming landscape. They are inconsolable.

Me, too.

Mom and the Waitress

My mother's birthday was last Sunday, March 5. She died eight years ago, but I think about her nearly every day, especially when I comb my hair, which is thinning at my left temple for some reason I can only ascribe to aging. I hope it doesn't worsen, but we shall see. My husband, father, and younger brother are all bald, and it's a fine look on them, but I'm not sure it'd be a good one on me.

Speaking of hair, I love one particular picture I have of my mother from when she was a young woman. I think it's her college graduation picture. She is unsmiling in her sweater and single strand of pearls, but her springy, wavy hair captures an innate liveliness not always obvious at first glance. Her hair, strawberry blonde, initially fading to a more reddish brown, thinned as the years passed, but it never grayed.

When I was a child, my hair was blonde, not the pure white of some Scandinavians, or the buttery yellow of my pal Connie's tresses, but more golden, like a lion's mane. When I was a young adult, my hair was still blonde, shot through with streaks from a searing sun that bleached my long locks during the summers over which I loved a guy who lived in a house by the sea in Rehoboth Beach, Delaware. But now that I'm an older adult (to put it kindly) with thinning hair, describing my hair as even dirty blonde is a stretch. Still, I'd place it somewhere on the dark-blonde-to-light-brown continuum. However, once Alzheimer's grabbed hold of my mother's once-nimble mind and refused to let go, she often asked, "When did your hair get so black?"

I am embarrassed to admit that fairly innocuous question made me furious. I would huff and puff with enough ire to blow a house down. How stupid! I suspect my anger had nothing to do with my hair and everything to do with not feeling fully seen, known, understood, or accepted by my mother for decades. Then, just when I was finally letting go of all my resentment towards my mother, Alzheimer's blew in and slammed the door shut on any kind of close mutual relationship she and I may have been able to forge later in our lives. Now, that's something to be mad (and sad) about.

Back to the black. On a Sunday afternoon, after the 10:30 service at the First Presbyterian Church in the old mill town of Gloversville, New York, which my mother has attended for more than fifty years, and where well-meaning churchy people cooed over her like she was a baby bird, making me inwardly cringe, we filed into the Holiday Inn's restaurant, sprightly named "Spirit," in nearby Johnstown. After listening to Linda, the waitress, expertly reel off the specials, my parents ordered what they always did. Well, my mother just sat there, and my father ordered for them both: fish, a healthy choice, not that the omega fatty acids mattered much at that point for my mother's gummed-up brain.

We didn't wait long for our food. The restaurant was not even half-full, and Linda was a conscientious waitress. No entrées grow cold, waiting for pickup while she is on duty.

"What's the black?" asked my mother, pointing to the grill marks on my father's salmon. My father and I exchanged uneasy glances. She would not eat anything that had "black" on it. In the next moment, Linda diverted my mother's attention when she set a plate down in front of her with that unique flourish only seasoned waitresses can pull off. "Here's your meal, Betty."

The colors on the pale, porcelain plate caught my eye: pink, white, and orange—and then I smelled the salmon, poached not grilled, potatoes mashed with any chunks of skin removed, and carrots undressed, without any parsley, all traces of anything my mother would label as "black," removed. Would she eat it or fuss about "black" specks, traces, or other marks on her food that often only she could see?

Alzheimer's reduced her once robust vocabulary to a few catch-all words. I was curious about her fixation on *black* in moments when I was not wracked by grief over my mother's progressive diminishment. Alzheimer's reduces us all in so many ways. I was often an awkward, mute presence in my mother's company. I did not know how to reach her or if she even wanted to connect with me. I pictured us on opposite ends of one of those scary rope bridges, swaying high up in the Himalayas, unable to take a few steps forward, let alone meet in the middle.

As I watched what was clearly a routine play out between Linda and my parents, I dared to exhale. My mother picked up her fork and started to eat her meal. I didn't even know I was holding my breath.

After dessert and coffee for my parents, and after my father paid and slipped a generous tip into the faux-leather check holder, we shoved our chairs back from the table and hauled ourselves up, bellies stuffed and bulging. My pants felt snug.

Linda pulled me aside as we filed out of the dining hall. "I just want to tell you how much I love waiting on your parents," she said. For a moment, a blessed moment, her kindness pierced my grief.

Love You,
Sweetie

Every day, around 3 p.m., Dad calls my older brother, Bill. He's been doing this ever since Mother died, and he moved twenty-nine miles east, leaving his home of over fifty years for a retirement community in Saratoga Springs, New York. Dad and his kids all feel better with a daily check-in. He is often quite jolly in these calls. "Not pushing up daisies, yet," he jokes on the phone to my brother. In his nineties, he doesn't take life for granted. "Never buy green bananas," he tells me with a hint of amusement in his voice. I love my father's sense of humor.

I am the back-up kid. Dad only calls me when Bill travels, which he frequently does, far and wide, on Mediterranean and Caribbean cruises and weeks in South Africa and Vietnam and India, where he rode high atop an elephant.

Mostly, when Bill is away, Dad remembers to call. But on occasion, he forgets, and then I worry, a nagging little fret at first, which gathers momentum over the hours that I don't hear from him until it explodes into a full-blown anxiety attack by early evening. Once, when Dad didn't call when he was supposed to, and after I called his phone and didn't reach him, I rang the front desk at the community where he lives in a one-bedroom apartment with Sparky, the fat cat, and told the security guard my concerns, punctuating my worry with little bursts of nervous laughs, as I am wont to do. The guard used a soothing tone to try to allay my fears and said, "I'll go knock on his door," which is exactly what he did after he took the slow elevator to the second floor.

When my father didn't answer, the guard reported that he turned the master key he carries on a chain in his pocket and opened the door, and Sparky arose from a nap, stretched long, and greeted him, rubbing up against his legs, marking him as friend, not foe. And since there was no dead, moldering body in the apartment and the lights were on, the guard called me back and told me about the cat and that he figured my father was okay and at some activity, which turned out to be the case (a movie, Wes Anderson's *The Grand Budapest Hotel*, of which Dad was not a fan).

Since then, and gradually over time, Dad attends fewer and fewer evening movies in the complex, even ones I know he would like, like Steven Spielberg's exceedingly intelligent *Bridge of Spies*. I've asked him about this drop-off, and we've identified two main reasons for the decline: He gets winded pushing his walker to the venue, and he has trouble staying awake through the film (a state I succumb to during anything animated). We agree that old age isn't for sissies.

I am always delighted to hear from my father. Sometimes, I feel guilty I am not nearby to pop in and see him. I live off the coast of Central Florida, by the ocean, and he lives in upstate New York, near Lake George and several mountain ranges, which rise up in the distance, making me feel grounded and solid as a statue of marble when I visit. Sometimes, I fear that I am a bad daughter—not for lack of caring or expending a ton of psychic energy worrying about him (if there were a prize for most neurotic worrier, I would certainly deserve at least honorable mention)—but for not fulfilling my daughterly duties. Isn't it usually the daughter who cares for the elderly parents? Isn't it the daughter who ferries the folks to doctor appointments? Isn't it the daughter who does the pop-ins?

That hasn't been the situation in our family. Instead, Bill has done a yeoman's job of caring for our parents as a couple and now for our father as a singlet. He took Dad grocery shopping at Walmart and Price Chopper for years until Dad decided he no longer wanted to go. Bill drives up the Northway from his home in Albany to Dad's (about thirty-two miles) to take him to medical appointments, and sits in while the doc calmly listens to my father when he interrupts her (many times), and then picks up exactly where she left off. Bill once wrote in an email, "The doctor should be a candidate for sainthood."

We all agree, including the pater, that he hates to cede control. Who doesn't? Combine that with a healthy skepticism, as well as a borderline-paranoid opposition to medical intervention, and he's one tricky (or maybe typical?) patient. But he's also pretty likable, with an exceedingly robust sense of humor and a kind and generous nature. For non-family members, I bet those traits outshine any old-man crabbiness.

Living far away as I do, and watching time pass as it does, with the almost imperceptible seasonal changes here in Florida—which I notice mostly by how the light changes around dinnertime so that I have to adjust the blinds to comfortably read the newspaper sitting at the dining room table while I wait for Jim to come home from work, and how the sea grape leaves curl up and turn brown around the edges—sometimes, I don't feel like I'm living up to my daughterly duties. But the truth is, I've never played that role. I left home for college and didn't give a moment's thought to living there after graduation—and my parents never encouraged me to move back. I've visited over the years, mostly because I wanted to and not because I felt obligated. The visits were punctuated like bookends: I was glad to arrive and glad to leave. I bet my parents felt the same. We all had full, separate lives (and still do).

And the reality is that Dad does not want to talk to me every day. Some days, he just wants to do his duty, complete his check-in, leave a message on the answering machine, and sign off with "Love you, Sweetie."

I get it. We are a family of introverts. Every single one of us is an introvert, if I was accurate in my administration and interpretation of the Myers-Briggs Type Indicator with my family a few decades ago. My friend Nedra once said I was the "good" kind of introvert. I think she meant I have decent social skills, and I would say that is true of my family members. We are not antisocial, and we enjoy the company of people in controlled, limited doses. For my father, that's about forty-five minutes of exercise twice a week on Tuesdays and Thursdays, two hours of *Trivial Pursuit* on Wednesday afternoons with a couple of ladies up a floor, two hours of *Upwords* on Saturdays in the community room, participating in two different book groups, and showing up as the occasional fill-in for bridge. All that activity strikes me as actually quite a lot of people-stuff for an introvert.

Still, I wish Dad would hang out on the phone more with me. Am I greedy that I want more of my father? Indeed, he feels ever more precious to me as we age. I want to suck in every moment I can while he is still here—although, in some of our calls, he isn't really fully there. He doesn't want to hear about the cats, or my friends, or about the minutiae of my life. He sounds winded, or I feel his congestion in *my* throat, and I know immediately he doesn't want to stay on the phone with me. His impatience makes me jittery. And, if he has an appointment or a commitment, even if it's hours away, he is often too anxious or preoccupied to settle into a few focused minutes with me.

So, the phone calls are not always as connected as I'd like. Yet, there is something so important, so vital, so valuable to have my father there on the other end of the line—however incompletely. Who doesn't want to hear, "Love you, Sweetie?" That love-thing transcends all else, doesn't it?

Recently, on a Wednesday, I broke our protocol and called my father around 3:45 p.m. I'd missed his calls for the last three days while my brother cruised the Caribbean. I wanted to talk to Dad before I went to the beach to spear bits of plastic and cigarette butts and check for baby turtles washed back on the browning seaweed that lined the beach since terrific storms like Matthew and Nicole churned the seas.

We exchanged our pleasantries. Dad said he was eating some lentil soup but that he could warm it up when we were done talking. I said, "How long do you think you're going to be around? Do you think you're going to live to be one hundred?"

He didn't act surprised at all by my question, one that some would find impertinent, and after setting his cooling cup of soup to the side, said, "I don't know. You know, I've got that damn leaky aortic valve."

"Remind me how that affects you," I say.

He says, "It's mostly energy, a lack of energy." He talks, too, for a few minutes about broken sleep during the night and the frequent desire to nap during the day, blaming it on medication for high blood pressure. He adds quickly, "I'm still mentally sharp."

I concur. "How much do you weigh these days?" I ask.

He says, "135 pounds."

I say, "Please don't go any lower than that."

He tells me he was up to 160 at one point, but that was a while ago, a long while ago.

Then I say, "I like to get as much of you as I can." It's my equivalent of "Love you, Sweetie," but at the beginning of the conversation, not the end. And on this day, he settles in for a spell with me on the phone, and we discuss Hillary and Trump, always *Hillary* and *Trump*, never *Clinton* and *Donald*. We admit our fear of a President Trump, and in that shared admitting, my own fear subsides just a tad. There is something so powerful in naming it—just naming the fear with someone who feels the same, or at least understands it. Maybe that's the appeal of my craving my father—those moments of resonance when I feel in every cell of my body that we are on the same wavelength.

I tell him about my efforts to canvass for Hillary and the problems I encounter: hostile neighbors, organizers on vacation, and incomplete training—and my fear about walking in unfamiliar neighborhoods in a state that has more guns than Texas. I probably could have omitted that little nugget about firearms, but it just popped out.

I hope I don't set him to worrying. He and I share a tendency to fret, to try to control the uncontrollable. I say, "I voted early. I was paranoid I was going to make a mistake and checked the ballot not once, not twice, but three times." He says something about me having OCD (obsessive-compulsive disorder).

I stifle a snort and think to myself: *The apple has not fallen far from the tree.* I tell him I was emotional voting, that I teared up, and that it surprised me. I think there's more woman-stuff here than I was even aware of. It's painful to see such denigration of women fomented by a candidate for president. But I think what scares me even more, is how distant I feel from my neighbors who support Trump and how they may feel the same way about me. It also scares me that we are so dualistic these days. Is there still an underlying fabric of unity? Was there ever? How do you have perspective while in the middle of change so completely disorienting? What is my responsibility as a "good" citizen? What is mine to do (or not to do)?

I tell him Jim has agreed to go with me on Sunday to canvass, even though he doesn't want to. Jim is a good guy. Come to think of it, he's a lot like my father, good-humored but sometimes emotionally distant. Perhaps that shouldn't be a surprise. I've often heard over the years from some amorphous "they" that you marry a version of your parents.

I can tell I am pushing my father's limits for phone conversation. I can feel his impatience starting to build. I imagine he is fidgeting in his poorly padded, cat-hair-covered chair, so we bring our conversation to a close. We end in our usual way.

"I'll talk to you soon. Love you, Dad."

And he says, "Love you too, Sweetie."

And, because you never know what could happen, given leaky valves and old age and deranged voters, I'll be sure to keep at least one of those "Love you, Sweetie" voicemail messages from my father on the answering machine for all the rest of my days.

Three Bras and a
Bottle of Bombshell

Yesterday, I did something I don't usually do—I shopped at Victoria's Secret. I didn't mean to. It just sort of happened.

The plan for the morning was to drive over the causeway to the library on Merritt Island, about twenty-five minutes away, to evaluate a new student for literacy services. This, because, after exploring a wide range of opportunities, I recently signed up to volunteer with Literacy for Adults in Brevard (LAB). After attending a couple of live workshops, spending a day getting certified to administer a standardized test (which brought back all my testing anxiety with a vengeance: shaky hands, flop sweat, heart palpitations), suffering through a slew of confusing back-and-forth emails with a variety of personages in the LAB office, playing phone tag with the student, and spending umpteen number of hours questioning my ability to fulfill my volunteer duties—despite having more than a decade of teaching and tutoring experience—and worrying about every single solitary thing that could possibly go wrong or right or *might* happen, I was set to meet him at the library at 9 a.m.

After making a screechy, death-defying left into on-coming traffic, I pulled into the library's parking lot. It was 8:38. By 8:40, I was sitting on the lone bench in the side yard, watching a squirrel pulse its tail and smelling freshly mown grass. At 8:58, I joined two older men and a teenage boy with tufts of purple hair framing his head-phones, outside the front door, where we commiserated about the sticky heat. At the stroke of 9:00, we rushed into the chilled air of the library lobby when the auto-matic doors whooshed open.

After I stopped by the front desk and scoped out the room I'd reserved, I sauntered back to the lobby to wait for my student. He was to identify me by my red purse, and I was to identify him by his handlebar mustache. I was sure we would find each other without difficulty. But alas, no student bounded over the threshold and through the automatic doors. At 9:10, I called him, got his voicemail, and left a message saying I hoped he was on his way, and if not, to please call me as soon as he could to let me know what was going on.

Then I plopped down on the couch in the lobby to wait. I said, "Good morning," to old coots, young men, middle-aged women, and young mothers trailing kids and pushing strollers. Every time the doors opened, I looked up expectantly. At 9:45, I gave up and bid adieu to Veronica at the front desk and drove a few miles to the mall, with the car windows open and the A/C off to chase away the library chill.

Plan A morphed into Plan B, with a new destination: LensCrafters. Since cataract surgery in January, I'd been making do without prescription sunglasses and, instead, pulling cheap, plastic frames with gigantic, polarized lenses over my new specs whenever I ventured out into the blinding Florida sun. The day before, I'd dropped the makeshift sunglasses on the floor, and even though the handy spouse had snapped the wayward lens back into place, I felt their days were numbered. So, after seeking guidance from Gaylene at LensCrafters and using a coupon they sent me for my birthday, I ponied up $303 for a new pair of Ray-Bans with progressive lenses. The store would text me when they were ready for pickup.

That's when I wandered into Victoria's Secret, directly across from LensCrafters. I immediately felt ill at ease, surrounded by tables and racks of panties and bras. I'm not sure why. After all, I've been wearing panties and bras for many decades, but generally not the lacy, frilly, see-through type spilling out all over the store.

A sales lady rushed to help, and I took a step back when she said, "Do you need bras? I'm a professional bra fitter, here from another store." Back home, my chest of drawers is filled with bras I don't wear, but at that moment, I found myself thinking, *Well, maybe I do need bras.* However, the thought of baring my breasts in front of this lady and letting her see the crummy, once-white-but-now-faded-gray bra I was wearing, complete with large safety pins to keep the straps in place, was more than I could bear at the moment. So, I just nervously laughed and started pawing at a rack of stretchy tights. The bra fitter hovered nearby, so I asked her about the tights. "What size do you think I'd wear? I'm thinking a medium." She concurred and then said, "Let me give you a coupon for a pair of panties" and rushed off to fetch the coupon.

Twenty minutes later, I left with my pink-and-cream Victoria's Secret bag stuffed with three pairs of tights, a pair of polka-dot panties, and a VS towel (complimentary, for spending more than $75), which I paid for with my plain old Visa card and not the Angel card they wanted to sell me, even though it would have given me an additional $15 off my order.

Then my phone buzzed. My Ray-Bans were ready.

The next day, in between munching on popcorn and kissing Cody on his cute little cat head, he and I read an article in *The New York Times* titled "Steady Paycheck, Shaky Income, Rising Angst." The story described how hard it is for a large swath of the population to find stability because they work jobs with ever-changing schedules. One of the profiled employees worked at a Victoria's Secret in Ocala, about seventy-five miles west of us, which is sometimes described as "horse country." But I suspect this employee does not keep horses. She makes $10 an hour, and sometimes is scheduled fifteen hours a week and sometimes thirty-nine, and it can change with little notice. When asked if the company provides benefits, she says it does, and I crossed my fingers, hoping she'd say they contribute toward healthcare or retirement. But here's what she says: "We're given three bras and a bottle of Bombshell, their number-one selling perfume."

I snort, "Well, whoop-de-do!" and startle the cat. I feel outraged on the employee's behalf. I fume: When did the bond break between employers and employees? I silently count my lucky stars *again* that I worked at the places I did, most that acted like they gave a shit about their employees and provided decent leave and benefits, including tuition reimbursement in return for dedicated service. My kneejerk reaction is to scratch Victoria's Secret off my list, but that's pretty much an impotent gesture—unlikely to help those I want to help. So, for now, I'll do what I do when troubled. I'll file it away until Jim comes home from work. Then I'll share it with him, listen to what he has to say, and either gain clarity or tuck it away in that place where I store things that require something, but I don't know what—yet—and wait until I do.

A Sunday Evening
with Dad

At about 4:45 p.m. on the Sunday before Thanksgiving, Dad and I start the trek from his second-floor apartment to Georgia's, the restaurant on the first floor of his retirement complex. It is no small feat, given his age (old), his mobility (limited), and his energy level (variable). He scrapes the apartment door with his walker before the door slams shut, leaving Sparky, the cat, hunched over his food; my brother, Bill, watching TV; and my husband, Jim, updating Dad's computer. The elevator pings, and Dad and I climb aboard. As we stand there waiting for the doors to inch ever so slowly closer together, we read aloud the flyers on the elevator wall advertising upcoming events—movie nights: *Rocky*, *The Deer Hunter*, *A Monster Calls*; a social with donuts and cider; and the Wesley residents' November birthdays. No Wrinkled Ramblers this month, but I bet the husband/wife duo will be back soon singing jaunty tunes and strumming on their old banjos.

Once a month, Dad participates in two different book gatherings, including the one tonight, the Consciousness-Raising Book Group. It meets at 6 p.m., and at 5 p.m., he routinely treats the leader, Reverend Joanne, a minister of Religious Science, and her close friend Carolyn, another Wesley resident, to dinner.

Dad likes to be early, and so we are—it takes us five minutes to get there, not the fifteen he insisted on leaving to compensate for all possible contingencies associated with maneuvering through the empty hallways. Outside the restaurant, he half sits, half falls into a chair near the other walkers lined up against the wall to wait for our guests. Carolyn and the good Rev show up right on time, and we tread in a single file behind Dad to a table in the corner.

Generally, an hour for dinner is plenty. But tonight, service is slow, even by Georgia's relaxed standards, and at 5:40 p.m., we are still waiting for our entrées: fish for three of us and something called Dutch beef for Carolyn. Dad is fretting and has said several times, "We'll have to get take-out containers, since we won't have time to finish eating before book group."

I stifle exasperation and keep myself from saying, "Dad, chill, Reverend Joanne has this." But I see I don't have to say anything. Reverend Joanne *does* have this. Their considerate comments and thoughtful questions clearly show they like and respect Dad. His fretting doesn't trigger anyone but me.

I hope that, in the final analysis, people will comment on the good I tried to do and not my oft-pervasive miasma of fret and anxiousness. Still, truthfully, the apple doesn't fall far from the tree—although, come to think of it, neither of my sibs overcompensate with time the way Dad and I do. Bill is freakishly punctual, almost to the dot, and could be described simply as reliable and steady. Tom, though? After years of waiting, we can count on Tom to be late, and he rarely disabuses us of that notion. Tonight, he is supposed to show up at 7:15 p.m., after book group, for a visit. However, Jim, with the detachment of an in-law, has already asked, "Who wants to wager how late Tom is going to be?"

It's so easy to see the fault in others, isn't it? Like the high fret and lack of proportionality my father is demonstrating right now. I can feel his anxiety—and have to consciously, and with effort, just let it go.

Then I see the waiter heading towards us with our food. Hooray! He sets down the plates of food, which are covered with clear domes of plastic to trap the heat, near Carolyn, and then distributes them. I dig into my rice, overcooked halibut, and mushy Brussels sprouts. I note (silently), for at least the tenth time, that this kitchen overcooks the food. I mention this to Jim later, and he says, "I wonder if they do that to make it easier for the residents to chew." I wonder, too—one of life's little mysteries.

As it turns out, fifteen minutes is long enough for three of the four of us to finish our meals. Dad, a notoriously slow eater, packs the two-thirds he hasn't consumed into the grungy, plastic Tupperware container he has brought down in the compartment in his walker. I dash into the restroom for a quick pee and floss and am distressed to see I have lettuce in my front teeth. That means that through the whole dinner-waiting conversation, I was speaking with green teeth. I wish someone had said something. But it's not a big deal. I tucked floss into my bra earlier, and now snap off a thread and quickly remedy the situation.

At 6 p.m., Reverend Joanne promptly starts the book group with introductions. Donna, Rick, my father Bill, Carolyn, Ilene, Rose, and I have gathered to discuss Emmett Fox's *Power Through Constructive Thinking*. Reverend Joanne hands out a list of questions with specific quotes, pages, and paragraph numbers cited, and it is easy to follow along—even for me, who hasn't finished the book. It's not for lack of effort, but because I misjudged how slowly it would go. This book is not a quick read. It was written in 1932, with a kind of old-timey language, and it quotes the Bible liberally, which for me has never been an easy read.

Fox discusses the Bible, but from a relatable and palatable metaphysical perspective. He says in his introduction: "The teaching in this book is founded on the Bible. The Bible is not like any other book; it is a spiritual vortex through which spiritual power pours from heaven to earth, and the reason why most people derive comparatively little profit from its study is that they lack the spiritual key." He goes on, "You can have power to make your life healthy, happy, useful, and outstandingly successful, if you will study the laws of life, and apply them faithfully."

I especially like the spiritual-vortex part. That makes sense to me if I think of spiritual power as a type of vibrational energy.

A robust discussion follows about realigning our thinking, the power of regular prayer and meditation to lift our consciousness, the tricky ways the ego trips us up, and the recognition and acceptance of our own divinity. I sigh at one point, profoundly sad at all the time I've wasted being so humanly me. I sigh, feeling the weight of all my faults and resistance to what seems abundantly clear sitting around the table with these fellow seekers—all the good right here in front of me in the perfect now, the possibility of living life on life's terms without making *everything a big deal*, and how I yearn to break free from the cage of our fear-based culture.

But this is not the moment to linger in regret. Right now, in this moment, I am in a metaphysical-book group with five other ladies and two men, one my elderly father, whom I love with a fierceness that scares me sometimes and makes me fear I will crumble and blow away when he passes on, which can't be all that far away, given that he is old. But right now, he is alive and sitting next to me on a darkling Sunday night in Saratoga Springs, with a lovely group of spiritual human beings, sharing insights and our daily challenges to transcend all the big and little problems of modern-day life.

Reverend Joanne brings us to a close promptly at 7 p.m. As we start the trek down the long hall and back to the elevator, Dad says, "I feel like I spoke too much, as always."

I say, "It didn't seem so to me. It seemed everyone appreciated what you had to say." I think, for the hundredth time, what a good professor he would have been—funny and humble, overly prepared and diligent. I think, for the hundredth time, how easy it is to see the magnificence in everyone else. I wonder: Why do we seem to be designed with that blind spot when it comes to ourselves?

Back in the apartment, Dad sinks into a worn chair, mostly devoid of any structural support. Bill, Jim, and I take our customary seats in the living room, settling in, to wait for Tom, making a side trip to see us on his way to pick up daughter, Mary, from college for the holiday break. I check my phone and see a cheery text from my sister-in-law: *Hi. Tom has been at work all afternoon to make up for tomorrow's absence. He just left for Dad's.*

Ugh! While I appreciate Tom making an effort to see us, his tardiness means at least an additional two-hour wait for the rest of us who have already been together since mid-afternoon. This family of introverts is fast approaching their max for togetherness; everyone is getting tired. I groan, complain loudly, like I am about five years old. I can't do a thing to change this specific situation other than to leave, and we aren't going to do that. We want to see Tom.

Here's an idea. What if I practiced what I was just immersed in for an hour with Fox's teachings? Worth a shot. So, I give my body a little shake to fling off the irritation hanging on, and I make a conscious decision not to get sucked down the same old rabbit holes of criticism and judgment and wanting circumstances to be different than they are.

Together, we watch *60 Minutes* and then a funny episode of *Frasier* on Netflix. Dad's laughter ricochets around the entire living room, crowding out any of his daughter's fret about waiting for her younger brother. And when Tom shows up two hours later, at 9:22 p.m., I greet him at the door with a big, welcoming hug—and I mean it.

The Ice Bucket

In late January, the spouse and I embark on a rare mid-week, overnight trip. An *overnight* makes it sound like a camping trip, doesn't it? This excursion was far from that, although I have fond memories of camping as a Girl Scout at Camp Kowaumkami (said *kuh-wonk-uh-mee*) on Caroga Lake in the Adirondack Mountains. Scurrying from our lean-tos, named for various Native tribes—Chippewa, Seneca, Mohawk, Iroquois—names carved into wooden plaques over the entrances, we gathered around the campfire to sing the camp anthem: "Camp Kowaumkami, we honor thee, friendship strong," blah, blah, blah. I have forgotten most of it, but remember a line about faith, hope, and charity. Or am I conflating the Camp K. anthem with our wedding vows?

This overnight is not to Caroga Lake, but Winter Park, north of Orlando, and specifically to the Alfond Inn, a swanky place reeking of good taste. We check in, slip upstairs in the speedy, quiet elevator, and find our room. We set our bags down with a soft *thud*, muffled by the thick carpet in our room on the fourth floor, decorated in cool blues and soothing greens. Contemporary art lines the silent hallways, and we sign up for the docent tour the next afternoon. A fire blazes in the library's fireplace. We plop down on the couch to stare at the flames. A clock ticks on the bookshelf. Two couples play bridge nearby, ice melting in their drinks, as they make their bids in hushed voices.

We are taking a bit of a chance staying here, as our habit regarding accommodations is to book a suite when we travel. We have significant snoring issues, and a second room allows for isolation of the snorer (that'd be Jim). But hotel options are limited in the area, and there are no suites available here. And we like the ethos of the place: The hotel donates part of its profits to nearby Rollins College's scholarship fund.

When I booked the reservation, I reasoned, surely, we could share a room for one night without incident. It's just one night. No big deal. Right?

After attending the event we came for, an opening of a Maya Lin exhibit at the nearby Orlando Museum of Art, we return to the hotel room, where Jim, exhausted, falls quickly into slumber. I have data to prove this. Recently, his Fitbit clocked his descent into dreamland at under a minute. I envy this talent of his, this seemingly effortless ability to tumble into sleep, which I do not share.

But this is my reading time, which I adore. I arrange the puffy pillows around me and open up *A Walk in the Woods*, always finding Bill Bryson enormously good company, especially when we travel, since that is when I gravitate to lighter reads. He's one of the few authors

(David Sedaris and Anne Lamott other favorites) who makes me laugh out loud, which he does tonight. I chuckle at his exasperation with Stephen Katz, his hiking partner. Never the most patient person on earth, I know exasperation well. And I've always entertained the notion that someday I, too, or Jim and I together, will hike the Appalachian Trail. However, as I read on and see what that endeavor *really* entails, a cold reality replaces my gauzy fantasy. I reach a good place to stop, close the book, insert my earplugs, reach over and turn on the sound machine, click off the light, and wait for sleep, which eventually comes.

Sometime later, maybe an hour, maybe two, despite the earplugs, despite the sound machine, I am jarred awake by Jim's snoring. Over the years, I've been a witness to a whole menu of his snores, ranging from the sudden pig snorts that levitate the cats straight up from the bed, to the soft whisper through pursed lips I first identified lying beside him and observing him like a subject in a lab experiment. Tonight, his noise is a droning, steady snore, just this side of a strangled moan.

Anger flares up and threatens to take hold; I do my best to shrug it away. It comes back. I flash on all those nights of broken sleep early in our marriage when I shrugged it away, too. Murder was not then, and is still not, a viable option. I love Jim when he isn't snoring. Can I love him when he is? I want to.

What to do? What to do? I consider getting dressed and going for a walk, but fear I'll be pegged as the village idiot wandering the streets in the middle of the night.

My mind rifles through the hotel's options. Aren't there plush, padded lounge chairs by the pool down on the second floor that might make for cozy snoozing? Alas, the pool closed for the night hours ago.

I am stuck in the room with snore-boy. My eyes alight on the bathroom, which is surprisingly spacious and might be a decent option. It is about as far away from the snorer as I can get and not be out in the hall. True, it has a cold, hard, tile floor—but no problem. I can cushion that with the plump, down comforter and oversized pillows from the bed. And, best of all, and this is key, the bathroom has a thick, solid door.

So, I sleep (sort of) on the bathroom floor in our expensive hotel room that night in late January. I'm not sure for how long, since any natural rhythms are disrupted by the bomb-shelter blackness of the windowless space. And by the way my eyes feel upon waking, gritty and dry, it isn't long enough.

I heave myself up and rub my stiff neck, shoulders, and left hip. It is hard to stand up straight. I note the bloodshot eyes staring back at me in the mirror. I slide open the bathroom door.

Jim is right there. We lock eyes. He looks scared, or at least alarmed, and like he is ready to bolt.

"Why didn't you wake me?" he asks and quickly adds, "I would have been happy to sleep in the bathroom."

I think to myself; *My body is ten times more flexible than yours*, and say, "Why should you sleep on the floor? It's not like you do it on purpose."

We are both surprised at my calm, measured response. We both stand up a little taller, and we exhale together, neither aware we'd been holding our breath.

He then adds, "Don't use the ice bucket."

What? My curiosity is piqued.

Turns out that the woman who didn't want to wake the man, so she slept on the bathroom floor, is married to a man who didn't want to wake the woman, so he used the ice bucket, careful to first line it with a plastic bag, as a makeshift toilet.

Before we check out, we are careful to dump the pee in the proper receptacle and throw away the plastic bag. Alongside a generous tip, we leave a note: *Be sure to wash the ice bucket.*

Gratitude

I owe thanks to so many for this book, and I'll start with my Aunt Celie, an indispensable champion of my writing. I had hoped to finish this collection before she died, but to my great sorrow, that did not happen. I will have to imagine the conversation she and I would have had after she read it. While she died from lung cancer, she and my mother suffered from Charcot-Marie-Tooth disease (CMT), a progressive, incurable disorder of the peripheral nerves that control muscles. To honor their legacy, all proceeds from the sale of this book will go to charities that support understanding and finding cures for CMT, lung cancer, or Alzheimer's disease.

I am grateful to Jamie Morris, my editor, coach, Tarot channel, and friend, who gave me fierce support and encouragement, professional expertise, and intuitive wisdom just when I needed it most. She helped me develop my voice, toss what was crap, revise, and then polish the pieces with potential—staying true to the yearnings of my heart and my overarching vision. She has dramatically improved this collection—no small feat.

Thank you, Tia Levings, who showed up in my life just when I needed her to shepherd this collection through everything that comes after the writing: proofing, designing, publishing, and marketing. It turns out that it is true; writing is the easier part of the whole process (at least for this author).

Two additional women merit special mention. Claudia Finley Lambdin and Nedra Weinstein have accompanied me on this long journey to publication and never once flagged in their support. And, Claudia, thank you for laughing and tearing up in all the "right" places while listening to my drafts.

I am so grateful to my brother, Bill; my father, another Bill (although always "William" to my mother); and my friend, Amy Siller. They stepped in immediately, without hesitation, when I asked them extremely late in the process to review areas of concern. They gave me wise counsel and sound opinions, invaluably helpful. It is probably clear to readers that I am, indeed, my father's daughter. Thanks, Dad, for all you've given me—especially a love of cats and an irreverent sense of humor. I love you to the very depths of the deep, blue sea.

Thank you, Janet Bowman, Susan Canada, Debbie Choquette, Bonnie Cole, Thayer Drew, Valerie Fiorillo, Chris Flowers, Kyle and Sarah Ford, Pat Ford, Susan House, Judy Leaver, Michael Mervosh, Anna Noack, Patti Okun, Sandra Smith, Holly States, Bara Vaida, Leslie VanKleeck, Wim Vanschel, Shelley Wallace, Janet Hall Whitcomb, and Linda Zern—consistent voices of encouragement over the years. I am grateful to many other friends, family members, and casual acquaintances, who, by their words or deeds, lit something in me that fueled my stories or helped me navigate the oft-boulder-strewn road of introspective writing or offered words of motivation just when I needed them.

Some of my best ideas have sprung unbidden while spearing others' garbage. Many thanks to our informal cadre of trash collectors who endeavor to keep Cocoa Beach beautiful!

I am grateful for our cats, three Cs of comfort, and almost unbearable cuteness: Cayce, Catsby, and, in particular, one-eyed, ailing Cody. Cody lay at my feet throughout much of the writing and revision of this book. In between cat naps, he'd be poking me with a paw to stop typing and feed him, or to let him out on the porch, or to let him back in again, or pet him and hug him and murmur sweet terms of endearment while he purred away. Cody made it abundantly clear that cat-needs wait for no woman, a good reminder that there is a whole, wide world outside of my head just inches away.

And, finally, biggest thanks to Jim, my first and most important reader (and listener). Jim, with unfailing good humor, keen insights, indispensable technical skills, and a generous spirit, sharpens my work and creates the conditions that allow me to do what I want: write. I love you.

Gems all of you, I treasure you now and forever.

About the Author

Beth writes personal essays and autobiographical sketches that draw on the experiences and feature the people she meets during her ordinary, day-to-day life. Beth crafts stories specific to those experiences and yet shot through with strands of shared DNA, and the shared pathos of our common humanity. She finds that being self-absorbed and caring deeply about others are not mutually exclusive.

For over a decade, she wrote film reviews for *Voice of the Hill*, *The Senior Beacon*, and *Washington Window*, where her ongoing feature, "Window on Film," won a writing excellence award. Her nonfiction articles, sketches, and essays have been published in *Voice of the Hill*, *Natural Awakenings*, *The Washington Post*, *The Orlando Sentinel*, *The Leader-Herald*, *Florida Today*, and in several *Space Coast Writers' Guild Anthologies*.

Beth is a graduate of Hood College, The George Washington University, The Johns Hopkins University, The Barbara Brennan School of Healing, and The Space Coast Health Institute. She has toiled as a strawberry picker, railroad-tie sales rep, bus girl, waitress, relocation specialist, director of personnel, plant personnel manager, employment and EEO manager, special educator and tutor, massage therapist and energy healer, and, last but not least, writer—home in the world at last.

Born in Baltimore, Maryland, she grew up in upstate New York, and was a longtime resident of Washington, D.C. She currently lives in Cocoa Beach, Florida, with her husband, Jim, and cats.

Visit Beth at BethLambdin.com